Relationship-Rich Education

Relationship-Rich Education

How Human Connections Drive Success
in College

Peter Felten and Leo M. Lambert

JOHNS HOPKINS UNIVERSITY PRESS   BALTIMORE

© 2020 Johns Hopkins University Press
All rights reserved. Published 2020
Printed in the United States of America on acid-free paper
9 8 7 6 5 4 3 2

Johns Hopkins University Press
2715 North Charles Street
Baltimore, Maryland 21218-4363
www.press.jhu.edu

Library of Congress Cataloging-in-Publication Data

Names: Felten, Peter, author. | Lambert, Leo M., 1955– author.
Title: Relationship-rich education : how human connections drive
    success in college / Peter Felten and Leo M. Lambert.
Description: Baltimore : Johns Hopkins University Press, 2020. |
    Includes bibliographical references and index.
Identifiers: LCCN 2020002995 | ISBN 9781421439365 (hardcover) |
    ISBN 9781421439372 (ebook)
Subjects: LCSH: College student development programs—United
    States. | Communication in higher education—United States. |
    Teacher-student relationships—United States. | College students—
    United States—Psychology. | College teaching—United States. |
    Interaction analysis in education—United States. | Education,
    Higher—Aims and objectives—United States.
Classification: LCC LB2343.4 .F45 2020 | DDC 378.1/98—dc23
LC record available at https://lccn.loc.gov/2020002995

A catalog record for this book is available from the British Library.

*Special discounts are available for bulk purchases of this book. For more
information, please contact Special Sales at specialsales@jh.edu.*

Johns Hopkins University Press uses environmentally friendly book
materials, including recycled text paper that is composed of at least
30 percent post-consumer waste, whenever possible.

To our parents, our earliest mentors:

Catherine Poehling Felten and Edward Felten
Yvonnette (Scotty) Gosselin Lambert and Paul Lambert

Contents

Foreword

You may have read the title of this book and thought to yourself, "Yes, of course, relationships *are* crucial to advancing student learning and success; we've known this for quite some time." If so, you may also be wondering what Peter Felten and Leo Lambert will offer in the pages that follow, whether reading them will be worth your while. Our reactions, we admit, were similar—with perhaps one exception: We have both worked closely enough with them to know they would only pursue this work if they believed it would both fill a gap in our knowledge base and lead us to more humane coexistence. And indeed it does.

The book's subtitle hints at what may be its most significant contribution; that is, an intentional shifting of the question from *whether* human connections drive college success to *how* they do so. By conducting nearly four hundred interviews at more than two dozen varied institutions, Felten and Lambert offer much-needed depictions of relationship-rich environments, telling and validating stories most of us would never have heard or perhaps never placed in their important context. In so doing, they have also enriched the scholarly record of contemporary higher education, adding a human element often relegated to the background, certainly today, when technology and analytics take center stage.

At the same time, this book makes clear that higher education leaders have not yet put meaningful human connections at the center of the undergraduate experience, despite evidence that has been mounting for more than forty years that relationships are crucial to students' success. And the authors do this without judgment and with great care, taking the time to identify and examine the challenge and to propose principles that will guide us.

Felten and Lambert advance our understanding of relationships by expanding the scope and implementation of previous work. Indeed, their conception of relationships is broad, nimble, and imminently (even surprisingly) practical. The richness of practices they discuss is alive in authentic course materials, assignments, and curriculum, classrooms, residence halls, laboratories, advising offices, and mentoring communities and conversations. The authors show us that relationships can be invoked in a convocation speech, used to inform the layout of a library, or relayed via the simple question "What's your story?"

We are reminded that our institutions are alive—they produce energy, and their parts work together and interact with one another at all times. What happens in one part influences all others—in service to health and well-being or to distrust, even disease. What becomes clear is that it all matters: how we interact, with whom we interact, and our intentions in our interactions with one another.

This book comes at a pivotal moment in our society and institutions. Many of our students express a deep desire for a sense of belonging on our campuses. There is much in our world that divides and disconnects us from our true values and makes it difficult to remember the very reasons for the journey in the first place. Notably, our student population in US higher education is more diverse than ever before. As the authors point out, more than 55 percent of undergraduates are women, 45 percent are students of color, and 40 percent are aged twenty-four or older. We know from experience and a growing body of research that students' sense of belonging and connectedness in higher education institutions is tied to essential outcomes, including their academic achievement, their well-being, motivation, and retention. This is the case for all students, regardless of their background, but particularly for first-generation and minoritized students.

Two important points here worth calling out explicitly are that this time of unprecedented diversity makes the centering of human connection more urgent than it has been for quite some time, and that doing so brings additional, often invisible, challenges. As Jan Arminio, Vasti Torres, and Raechele Pope have written, "learning through relationships with others" is a core pillar of advancing inclusion in colleges and universities, yet attaining inclusion will require that we transcend our human instinct to relate to those similar to us. "The tendency to associate with people most like us," Arminio, Torres, and Pope affirm, "is the opposite of inclusion and is the force to be contended with in building inclusive communities."[1] As such, we will need to be intentional about promoting connections among the diverse members of our communities, and we will each need to enhance our ability to relate to others, particularly across our ethnic and racial differences.

Contemporary higher education is also characterized by an increase in student stress levels and growing demand for more comprehensive approaches to the constantly evolving ways students experience the world. Here, too, we know from experience and research that relationships and connections matter. The Stanford Medicine Center for Compassion and Altruism Research and Education tells us that the absence of "social connection is a greater detriment to health than obesity, smoking and high blood pressure"; the center also describes the "positive feedback loop of social, emotional and physical well-being" that results from increasing human connection: "People who feel more connected to others have lower levels of anxiety and depression. . . . [T]hey also have higher self-esteem, greater empathy for others, are more trusting and cooperative and, as a consequence, others are more open to trusting and cooperating with them."[2] Note that this research refers to *people*, not simply to students. We *all* serve to gain from relationship-rich institutional cultures.

Felten and Lambert have devoted their professional careers to teaching and scholarship, as well as fostering student-centered cultures that value human connection. What you have before you is a testament to their professional work together, to their own relationship, and to the highly relational approach they took in their research, in an effort to understand the work of their colleagues around the country. Their gift to us is the gift of story, of heartwarming, vivid stories of human connection at its best. As you read, we hope you'll pause and relate the stories to the many rich relationships in your own experience and in your institutions, as we did. Celebrate when and where the work is being done well. The authors invite us to notice, and they give us permission to recognize and deepen the current relationships in our institutions—not to start from scratch, not to develop another initiative, but to live and work in relation to one another.

This book makes clear that everyone has a role in creating the kind of culture that lives up to the promise of higher education—to renew the democratic ethos that is woven into our institutions. That promise has everything to do with expanding opportunities for students, treating students well, educating citizens, and cultivating goodwill among communities. Our colleges and universities, after all, have heart. They are places where students from all backgrounds, ages, and identities come together to expand their knowledge, form habits, and prepare themselves for life in this century. Let us each commit to imbuing these places with authentic, plentiful, interconnected, compassionate relationships.

Isis Artze-Vega, Vice President of Academic Affairs,
Valencia College

Ed Taylor, Vice Provost and Dean of Undergraduate Academic Affairs, University of Washington

Acknowledgments

Writing this book would have been impossible without the powerful, illuminating stories about relationships in undergraduate education shared with us by nearly four hundred people—students, faculty, staff, college and university presidents, deans and administrators, and other thought leaders in higher education—representing more than two dozen campuses throughout the United States. We are in their debt for giving us a more detailed understanding about how relationships shape the undergraduate experience profoundly, as well as permission to use their voices to amplify key ideas with a special sense of authenticity.

We had the great privilege of making site visits to sixteen campuses to complete extensive interviewing and are grateful to many colleagues who arranged our itineraries and provided us with space to work and many other forms of hospitality, especially Mary Wright of Brown University; Alison Cook-Sather of Bryn Mawr College; Adriana Aldana and Ken O'Donnell of California State University–Dominguez Hills; Donna Linderman of the City University of New York; Isis Artze-Vega at Florida International University; Ashley Holmes at Georgia State University; Joanne Stewart and Cathy Mader of Hope College; Gail Mellow, Bret Eynon, and Robert Jaffe of LaGuardia Community College; Tony Scinta of Nevada State College; Joianne Smith and Jennifer Jennings of Oakton Community College; Timothy Eatman, Brian Murphy, and Peter Englot of Rutgers University–Newark; Paul LeBlanc and Morgan Smith of Southern New Hampshire

University; Andrew Beckett and Sarah Hansen of the University of Iowa; Ayeza Saddiqi, Michelle Ferrez, and Dilip Das of the University of Michigan; and Ed Taylor, Anne Browning, and Micah Trapp of the University of Washington.

Our thinking was also influenced by formal interviews with other leading thinkers and scholars of higher education: Mary-Ann Winkelmes of Brandeis University; Donald Harward and David Scobey of Bringing Theory to Practice; John Zubizarreta of Columbia College; Connie Book, Steven House, Rodney Parks, and Paula Patch of Elon University; Randy Bass and Febin Bellamy of Georgetown University; Gretchen McKay of McDaniel College; Harold Martin of North Carolina A&T State University; Gregory Hodges of Patrick Henry Community College; Mays Imad of Pima Community College; Mary Deane Sorcinelli of the University of Massachusetts–Amherst; Manda Williamson of the University of Nebraska; Bryan Dewsbury of the University of Rhode Island; W. Brad Johnson of the United States Naval Academy; Sharon Daloz Parks of Leadership for the New Commons; and Andru Anderson of Wheaton College. We admire the leadership and contributions that each of these individuals has demonstrated to make relationship-rich education a hallmark of the undergraduate experience on their home campuses.

This project would not have been possible without the dedication and skill of our administrative assistants, Robin Plummer in the Office of the President Emeritus and Christopher Sulva in the Center for Engaged Learning, both at Elon University. With the support of student workers Abigail Gross and Jane Williams, they checked the accuracy of hundreds of hours of recorded interview transcripts, double-checked permissions for the use of all quotations included in this book, and coordinated our travel and many other logistics. We are thankful for their personal investment in this work, as well as for their patience, good humor, and colleagueship.

Our Elon colleagues and friends Jon Dooley, Eric Hall, Jean Rattigan-Rohr, and Maureen Vandermaas-Peeler gave us the gift of two days of their summers of 2018 to think through an early outline for this volume and sketch out major themes. Jason Husser, associate professor of political science and director of the Elon Poll, collaborated with us to conduct the national survey of four thousand college graduates that we reference in this book. These friends, and hundreds more colleagues at Elon, remind us what a privilege it is to work in a university environment that treasures the importance of mentors in the lives of undergraduate students.

Lou Albert of Arizona State University, Betsy Barefoot of the Gardner Institute, Frank Shushok Jr. of Virginia Tech, Jillian Kinzie of Indiana University, Isis Artze-Vega of Valencia College, Dianna Shandy of Macalester College, and Jon Dooley and Tim Peeples of Elon gave us immensely helpful feedback on drafts of this manuscript. Countless other colleagues across the country and around the world helped us think through ideas that animate this book. We are grateful for each of those conversations.

Sandra Fields' editorial acumen was indispensable as we brought this volume to final form. This is the second book project she has edited for us, and her comments, questions, and thoughtful observations were consistently astute.

Vicki Siler, a wonderful colleague in Belk Library at Elon University, was helpful to us at every turn by securing resources we needed and providing valuable technical reference guidance. Michael Shepherd of campus technology support also gave us hours of skillful assistance.

We are grateful to the authors of the foreword, Isis Artze-Vega of Valencia College and Ed Taylor of the University of Washington. Their work inspires us every day. Having them as colleagues, mentors, and friends is a gift.

Our editor at Johns Hopkins University Press, Greg Britton, has offered us wise counsel at every step. We also appreciate the expert guidance of Greg's colleagues Juliana McCarthy, Kyle Gipson, and Hilary Jacqmin and copyeditor Jackie Wehmueller. We are thankful for the sustained focus of the Johns Hopkins University Press on scholarship about higher education.

We are grateful to the Board of Trustees of Elon University for their enduring commitment to the Center for Engaged Learning at Elon University and for the support of a yearlong sabbatical for Leo Lambert following the conclusion of his nineteen-year presidency there. The Elon board provides exemplary leadership for their commitment to engaged learning and nurturing one of the finest environments for undergraduate education in the United States.

Most of all, we are lovingly thankful for our spouses, Laurie Lambert and Sara Walker, who unfailingly encouraged us and were patient and supportive during extensive time away from home for research travel and throughout the writing process.

Relationship-Rich Education

Introduction

Human connection is the basis upon which learning takes place.
Relationships are essential because there is no learning without
relationships.

—Randy Bass, Georgetown University

Relationships are the beating heart of the undergraduate experience.
We know this to be true. The research on the significance of
relationships in education is clear and long-standing. We hear
that scholarship echoed in the stories alumni tell about their college
days and the peers, professors, and staff who shaped their
learning and their lives. Many people can recall specific faculty
and staff members, peers, advisors, mentors, and coaches who
profoundly influenced not only their time in college but also
who they have become after graduation.

In this book our premise is that these relationships should not
occur by happenstance or only for some students. Indeed, scores
of students we interviewed told us of moments when they were
one relationship, or one conversation, away from dropping out of
college. Relationships matter. This book is an invitation—and a
challenge—to place relationships at the center of undergraduate
education for all students. We will look through the lens of relationships
to re-envision everything from classroom teaching and
student success initiatives to institutional cultures and structures.

In our research for this book, we set out to systematically gather and analyze stories of relationship-rich undergraduate education. We interviewed 385 students, faculty, and staff at twenty-nine higher education institutions across the United States. Their stories provide the backbone of this book.

Holly Graff is a professor of philosophy at Oakton Community College in suburban Chicago.* She related how one day a new student visited her office and "said in a very hostile voice, 'I don't want you to stereotype me because I just got out of the Marines.'" She assured him that she would not, and she asked him to tell her more about himself: "He ended up telling me that he was really concerned and very apprehensive about being back at school. He wasn't sure what it would be like and if he would be successful." As they talked, he also told her about all of the books he had read as a Marine. "He left that one-on-one conference with an honors contract for my class, because it became clear he was actually more advanced academically in terms of philosophy than any other student in my class."

That story resonates with a central finding from decades of higher education research: student-faculty relationships are a primary factor in learning, belonging, and persistence. Professor Graff recognized the potential in a student who entered her office expecting to be treated poorly, and her warm welcome and high expectations transformed this interaction—and, ultimately, his time in college. Faculty are central to a relationship-rich education. Staff and peers are also crucial to student success. Karla Chinchilla, a student at LaGuardia Community College in New York City, recalls:

---

* We use the names of interview subjects as much as possible throughout the book. As we describe later in the introduction, we name only interview subjects who have granted permission to use both their names and their quotations. We use descriptors (such as "student" or "president") that were current when we interviewed people, in 2018 and 2019.

I will never forget meeting the Peer Advisor Academy program coordinator, Crystal Rivas, for the first time. It was a very formal interview, but what has stuck with me is when she asked, "What's your story?" To this day I love using that line myself with students. Crystal saw things in me that I didn't know I had. She observed me frequently and would say, "This is what I see, this is what I'm hearing, and this is what we can do." Crystal put me in positions that I wouldn't have put myself in, but she knew I could do it. Her constructive feedback and detailed approach are what led to me growing as a student, a mentor, and professional.

Inspired by that interaction, Chinchilla now is a student employee with the Peer Advisor Academy at LaGuardia. In that role, she works with many new students, including Jessica Taurasi, who returned to college in her mid-twenties after several years away from school. Taurasi, now a peer advisor herself, explains how important these relationships can be:

When I think of peer advising, I think about my first peer advisor, Karla, and how she changed my life. She gave me the resources I needed to be a part of the community and be part of the college. She assisted me with being part of the clubs that I wanted to be in and to be part of the Peer Advisor Academy as well, and motivated me in ways that no one else did. The first time we met she was welcoming. She was warm. I guess she saw a little bit of herself in me, and me in her.

The Peer Advisor Academy has created a self-reinforcing cycle that connects staff and students in an unfolding web of relationships that enrich the education of students across the institution. This multiplies the effect of individual interactions and allows peer-to-peer connections to magnify the work of faculty and staff, creating a relationship-rich environment for all students.

Higher Education Today

Programs like the Peer Advisor Academy and individuals like Professor Graff are essential to serve the needs of students across higher education. In the minds of too many people, the image of a typical college student remains that of the late nineteenth-century "college man" or, much less frequently, "college woman"—white, privileged, focused on extracurricular activities, and carefree.[1] In today's higher education, students and institutions cannot rely on late-night bull sessions in the dorm or lazy afternoons on the quad to supply the relationship-rich environments that students need and want. Today, more than 55 percent of undergraduates are women, 45 percent are students of color, and 40 percent are age twenty-four or older.[2] More than 50 percent of all undergraduates live at home, almost 40 percent attend community colleges,[3] nearly 40 percent attend more than one institution before graduation, and about 25 percent are both full-time students *and* employed full time.[4] A recent study of students at sixty-six two- and four-year higher education institutions in twenty states found that roughly three in ten of the students in the sample were food insecure within the past month, and approximately one in ten had been homeless in the past year.[5] In a national survey of undergraduates, almost 90 percent reported feeling overwhelmed by all they had to do (57 percent of those said they felt overwhelmed "in the past two weeks"), and roughly 40 percent reported feeling "so depressed it was difficult to function" at least once in the past year.[6] Relationship-rich experiences are crucial for all students and are particularly important for the success of first-generation college students and what some have termed the "new majority"[7] of undergraduates in the United States—those who bring significant capacities to college but also often face long-standing inequities and barriers to attaining their educational aspirations.[8]

Like student demographics, institutional and political contexts are changing rapidly. Funding for both public and private higher education has been reduced just as technological and policy changes have increased competition among institutions. Political polarization threatens to erode public trust in higher education and to magnify divisions among groups on campuses. Occasionally these tensions flair into open conflict,[9] but more often they encourage people to retreat to the seeming safety of banal ideas and homogeneous communities that leave many feeling alienated and isolated.[10] As Sadia Abbas, a Rutgers University–Newark professor, told us in an interview, the world faces "a global crisis of citizenship and sociality" that spills onto campuses and into classrooms, and that crisis can make relationship building a seemingly impossible dream. In this dynamic and difficult environment, we believe individuals and institutions must make relationship-rich experiences the center of undergraduate education. Relationships are the path to the learning, professional, and civic outcomes of higher education for our students. Even when budgets are tight, tensions are high, and calendars are full, higher education's guiding question should not be Can we afford to do so? but, rather, Can we afford *not* to do so?

Relationship-Rich Education

Decades of research demonstrate that peer-to-peer, student-faculty, and student-staff relationships are the foundation of learning, belonging, and achieving in college.[11] Students' interactions with peers, faculty, and staff positively influence the breadth and depth of student learning, retention and graduation rates, and a wide range of other outcomes, including critical thinking, identity development, communication skills, and leadership abilities. As higher education researchers Adrianna Kezar and Dan Maxey document, these effects are "particularly strong" for "students of color and first-generation college students."[12] Relationships in college also create powerful legacies that touch alumni lives for years after graduation.[13] These relationships need not fit the classical model of long-term, one-on-one academic mentoring to matter for students' learning and lives; indeed, as we explain in chapter 1, even "mentors of the moment" can have lasting influence through brief, meaningful interactions.

For some students, college already fulfills the promise of meaningful relationships. At many institutions, well-resourced programs and specially tailored initiatives, such as honors colleges and residential learning communities, immerse students in relational environments. We believe that these and an array of other relationship-rich experiences not only should be available to a privileged set of undergraduates but should be at the heart of college for *every* student.

In our research, we explored programs and institutions that focus on supporting students to create webs of relationships that will sustain them through, and beyond, college. We found that the key is not tasking each student with identifying a single mentor who will meet all of their needs, but rather creating a relationship-rich environment where students will have frequent opportunities to connect with many peers, faculty, staff, and others on and off campus. One-on-one mentoring is powerful, yet it is expensive to structure and nearly impossible to scale to all students[14]; relationship-rich environments, on the other hand, are a flexible and affordable means to connect *every* student to the transformative ends of higher education.

Doing this work well is not easy but is possible at every institution and for every student. Individuals and institutions will need to rethink practices, policies, and priorities. The mantra echoing through this volume is that higher education must act so that all students experience welcome and care, become inspired to learn through interactions in and out of the classroom, cultivate constellations of important relationships, and use those relationships to explore the big questions of their lives. To influence every student in these ways is an enormously aspirational goal, but if students are to achieve the promise of higher education, no one in higher education can settle for anything less than relationship-rich experiences for all.

In order to meet that aim, institutions need to focus on the students right in front of them today as well as plan for the students they will serve tomorrow.[15] See them. Listen to them. Encourage them. Challenge them. In this book, you will come to know students, faculty, and staff—as well as programs and research—who do just that.

Our Research

In our research for this book, we did *not* replicate the vast empirical literature on how college affects students.[16] Instead, we collected and analyzed narratives and examples of relationship-rich education from diverse students and institutions across the country. To identify where to go and who to talk to, we wrote to 236 higher education thought leaders—college and university presidents, higher education foundation executives, scholars of undergraduate education, and faculty and staff who have been honored for their innovative work—to ask them a question: Which people, programs, and innovative practices across the spectrum of American higher education have most inspired you of late? We received a total of 84 responses (a 36 percent response rate), highlighting scores of exemplars.

Based on these nominations and our own knowledge of US higher education, we visited sixteen diverse campuses, which included community colleges, research universities, liberal arts colleges, a technical college, comprehensive public institutions, and a large online university. Our visits typically were scheduled for one and a half days on campus, allowing us to meet with many students, faculty, and staff for interviews both individually and in small groups. We visited these campuses:

Brown University
Bryn Mawr College
California State University–Dominguez Hills
CUNY–New York City College of Technology (City Tech)
Florida International University
Georgia State University
Haverford College
Hope College
LaGuardia Community College
Nevada State College
Oakton Community College
Rutgers University–Newark
Southern New Hampshire University (online campus)
University of Iowa
University of Michigan
University of Washington

In addition, we interviewed thought leaders either in person or by telephone at the following institutions and organizations:

Brandeis University
Bringing Theory to Practice
Columbia College (South Carolina)
Elon University
Georgetown University
McDaniel College
North Carolina A&T State University
Patrick Henry Community College
Pima Community College
United States Naval Academy
University of Massachusetts Amherst

University of Rhode Island
Wheaton College (Massachusetts)

Prior to each interview, participants gave written consent to be interviewed and recorded, following a research plan approved by the Elon University Institutional Review Board. All interviews were recorded and later transcribed. We lightly edited quotations for the book to enhance clarity by removing nonlexical vocables and smoothing out grammatical constructions. We received secondary consent from participants for every quote we use and for every time we name an interview subject.

Our interviews generated many hundreds of pages of transcripts. We analyzed these transcripts by drawing on our disciplinary training as a historian (Peter) and a higher education scholar (Leo), mining for the gems of emergent themes and powerful stories. We use these voices and narratives to illustrate and illuminate, and we rely on existing scholarly literature to make specific claims about the outcomes of relationship-rich education.

Of our 385 interviews, 204 were of undergraduate students. We collected demographic data on student interviewees to compile the following composite profile:

Median age: 23 (range 18–69)
Gender identity: 67% female, 32% male; 1% nonbinary

Number	Race/ethnicity
114	White
47	Hispanic or Latinx
31	Black or African American
28	Asian
10	Biracial or multiracial
2	Pacific Islander

(Interviewees could identify in more than one category.)

This Book

The book begins with two chapters that explore the power and challenges of relationship-rich undergraduate education. In chapter 1, we sketch visions of the possible, acknowledging the importance of context and the complexity of educational inter-actions yet making the case for four guiding principles in this work: all students must experience genuine welcome and deep care; relationships are a powerful means to inspire all students to learn; all students must develop webs of significant relationships in college; and all students need meaningful relationships to help them—and to challenge them—to examine the big questions of their lives.

Chapter 2 plunges into the difficulties of creating and sustaining relationship-rich education. These include the structures of institutions, such as the reward systems that ignore (and sometimes even punish) investments in time spent with undergraduate students, as well as the practical realities of student experiences, including when classrooms are sometimes less than engaging and stimulating. But often the primary difficulty lies with a lack of awareness of students' unseen burdens, including both the structural inequities that many students encounter in education and the personal feelings of doubt and fear that are cued in students by experiences on and off campus.

In chapter 3, we examine the importance of institutional culture to creating relationship-rich experiences for all. Student-centered campus culture is essential for relational education to flourish, which means that institutions must develop structures and practices that value students, recognize and reward the efforts faculty and staff devote to building relationships with students, value and practice excellent teaching, encourage all on campus to see themselves as part of a web of important interactions students will experience, and think critically about how metrics are used to assess student experiences as well as the work of faculty, staff, and administrators.

Chapter 4 focuses on the classroom, the single most important place for fostering undergraduate relationships. Across every institutional type, the classroom experience—which touches every student, often multiple times each day—can be dynamic and inspiring or dull and insipid. Active, engaged pedagogies can make all the difference in sparking important learning relationships among students and between students and instructors. Understanding the centrality of classroom experience to fostering relationships for all students on campus is essential.

Chapter 5 explores a diverse array of programs and intentional practices that cultivate relationships on campus, ranging from large-scale innovations in living-learning communities and course redesign to simple, grassroots practices that encourage students to use office hours, that build substantive connections between faculty and student athletes, and that encourage faculty, staff, and administrators to schedule time on their calendars to interact with students when traversing campus. We were struck again and again by the impact of these efforts for students—especially for first-generation or new majority students, some of whom are unfamiliar with the codes and traditions of the academy.

For chapter 6, we dig into the qualities of the many mentoring interactions students will have in college. Some of these relationships might be prompted by long and intense experiences such as conducting undergraduate research or sharing a small room in a residence hall. Our interviews suggest, however, that short-term, even one-time, "mentoring conversations" with faculty, staff, or peers also can be powerful and, occasionally, life changing. The key to creating a campus with a strong ethos of mentoring conversations is to empower all members of the campus community to conceive of themselves as being capable of the kinds of listening, encouraging, informing, and challenging that students need—and to raise their consciousness about how powerful their roles can be in guiding students during life's daily interactions in formal and informal settings on campus.

The book's conclusion offers strategic and practical advice for institutional and individual action. Listening to the inspirational ideas and powerful stories of 385 people was an immense privilege. Their voices echoed in our heads as we tried to think about the big questions: What does this mean? and How should higher education faculty, staff, and administrators act? It is our hope that the voices featured in this book will inspire readers to think carefully about their own context. Indeed, we hope this book inspires readers to see new possibilities in their students, their work, their institution, and across higher education. Looking through the lens of relationships offers a new vision of student learning and success.

Relationships are a flexible and adaptable approach to meeting the needs of diverse students. As Tianna Guerra, a student at Oakton Community College and an aspiring orthopedic surgeon, told us, "It only takes meeting that one great person who ignites a fire of passion within you." The central challenge of undergraduate education is guaranteeing that *every* student has the powerful human interactions that ignite that fire of passion. We believe every college and university can—and must—assure just that.

Chapter One

Visions of the Possible

When I came to college, I placed into the lowest math class, 060. With the help of Professor Borha and the inspiration that he gave me, I finished 060 and 070 in one semester and later became the math club president. He really started me off on the path of realizing that few are born geniuses and that if you want to learn and become great, it is through hard work, support, and dedication.

—Tianna Guerra, Oakton Community College

In our hundreds of interviews with students, faculty, and staff at more than two dozen colleges and universities, we heard many stories like Tianna Guerra's. Professor Mario Borha did much more than teach her math; he helped her to see a new vision of herself and her future. We begin this chapter with four brief stories, illustrating four of the most common themes we heard in our research—and suggesting visions of the possible for undergraduate education to be relationship rich for all students at all institutions.

Ivette Perez is a student at CUNY–New York City College of Technology, in the Accelerated Study in Associate Programs (ASAP), which focus on degree completion through intensive advising, clearly defined degree pathways, and financial support for transportation and books. In her initial interaction with her ASAP advisor, David Latimer, Perez says, "He welcomed me in a very warm way that I really didn't expect from an advisor or any staff member, because high school is kind of nonpersonal. And the first thing he said was, 'How are you today?' And that meant a lot to me, because not many people take the time to find out how you are doing."

Students on many campuses, from the most selective to open-access institutions, tell much the same story. College must require students to stretch and grow but need not be cold and impersonal. Students will struggle and stumble as they learn. To help them persist and succeed, institutions must provide consistent challenge and support to all students. That requires much more than a helpful orientation on their first day of classes. Instead, students need what David Scobey, director of the independent project Bringing Theory to Practice calls "relentless welcome." Students need to be interacting regularly with peers, faculty, and staff who ask them "How are you?" and genuinely listen to and care about their answers.

When José Robles, a nursing student at Nevada State College, enrolled in an introductory geology course he, like many students approaching their general education requirements, just wanted to "get out of here." Instead, something quite different happened: he fell in love with learning. "My professor made the course interactive in a way that something as boring as rocks became interesting. The passion she had, she wasn't just giving me information. Her subject was something that she loved. And the way that she explained it, for some reason, I wanted to learn everything about rocks. The most important thing is that the class became a community. She had us interact with each other and with the subject. It just came together because of her passion."

All students should have experiences in and out of the classroom that inspire them to learn more deeply and widely than they knew possible. Faculty are absolutely vital in this, but staff and peers also are pivotal in helping students to integrate the learning they do in their courses with their lives outside the classroom.

President Joianne Smith, a psychologist, leads Oakton Community College knowing that "belonging and having a sense of mattering allows individuals to thrive." But on a campus where every student commutes and 70 percent of students attend part time, she also knows that nurturing a sense of belonging must be an intentional, campus-wide effort. "Part of my vision for Oakton is that every student and employee feels that this is a place where they matter, where they belong, and where they're connected to someone—ideally more than one. Relationships are at the core of everything we do, and so creating inescapable opportunities for engagement is our focus."

Individual relationships can be educationally powerful, but a network of overlapping relationships is more likely to meet a student's evolving needs than any single mentor can. A web of student-student, student-faculty, and student-staff relationships creates a more resilient resource for a student to draw upon when the going gets tough—and offers institutions a more scalable approach to reaching every student, because faculty and staff can contribute their distinct expertise to support students.

LaGuardia Community College enrolls students from 160 nations speaking 120 languages, many not only being the first in their families to attend college but also managing complex lives involving jobs, families, and trying to escape from poverty. When President Gail Mellow of LaGuardia speaks of her faculty and their work in creating a curriculum, she says they knew careers were important, but they also had a bigger goal in mind. "Deep learning has to be meaningful. Our students are adults. They have to have learning that connects with who they are and who they are becoming as human beings. These students need to ask the big questions of their lives, and they need faculty, staff, and peer mentors to help them think through these questions."

Too often, the idea of college is reduced to a series of transactions, and the end point is narrowly seen as a ticket to a career.

Higher education should prepare students for work, of course; doing that, however, does not preclude the essential mission of prompting students to think critically and expansively about themselves, their communities, and the world.

Creating and Nurturing Relationship-Rich Environments

An undergraduate education that will carry value into the future is dependent upon students developing educationally purposeful relationships with faculty, staff, and peers. These relationships are both necessary and possible for every student at every type of institution: public and private, two- and four-year, highly selective and open access, traditional and online.

Some students—including those who have highly educated parents or who are extroverted and socially skilled—come to campus with a significant leg up on their peers in understanding both how the academy works and how to navigate relationships on campus. But meaningful human relationships, essential for undergraduate education to be as deep and powerful as possible, should be a reality for *every* student; they should be "inescapable" rather than optional, they should be available to all students rather than to a few students in select programs. For that to happen, institutions must commit to making relationship-rich undergraduate education a top campus priority. Ideally, the goal of relationship-rich undergraduate education will be embedded into institutional culture, but even if it is not, departments and programs and individual faculty and staff can still be powerful forces in seeding relational education within and across an institution.

The good news is that across the United States there are exemplary programs that connect students to peers, faculty, staff, and other potential mentors on and beyond campus. These programs require intentional design and execution, institutional champions at many levels, and supportive structures and policies. Programs, however, are not enough. Students also need to be immersed in an educational culture that values relationships and that nurtures webs of connections, including not only formal interactions with faculty and student life staff but also informal conversations with a wide range of staff, including dining-hall workers and campus custodians, who—we were told over and over again—provide critical, if unheralded, daily support for students.

In our interviews, we uncovered four interlocking relationship-rich principles that guide both effective programs and generative cultures at colleges and universities:

1. *Every student must experience genuine welcome and deep care.* All students need to understand that they are valued as people. This is prerequisite for their belief that they belong on campus, which is essential for persistence and academic success.

2. *Every student must be inspired to learn.* Students too often approach their educations as a series of transactions, hurdles to be cleared, and grades to be negotiated. Relationships help transform learning and motivation. All faculty members have opportunities to show genuine interest in students, share their passion for and expertise in their disciplines, and spark students to learn. Staff and peers are also crucial in creating communities that inspire learning in and out of the classroom.

3. *Every student must develop a web of significant relationships.* Many students may need to be coached and encouraged to take the initiative to build relationships with faculty, staff, and peers, whom they might initially view as intimidating or unapproachable. Institutional structures, like formal advising and mentoring programs, if done well, can serve

as catalysts by helping students build strong foundations for growing networks of educational relationships, but a web of individual actors is also essential to help students believe they belong and can succeed.

4. *Every student must explore questions of meaning and purpose.* College is a time for asking big questions about the world and about yourself. While this requires individual contemplation, for many students asking big questions is best done in conversation with people who care enough to take the time to listen generously and to encourage critical reflection. Pondering these questions with mentors, teachers, peers, and others with life experience to share provides the foundation for more practical explorations into majors, careers, and employment. Unless meaningful questions and relationships are at the heart of the college experience, students are likely to drift aimlessly.

Students are primary actors in all four of these principles. They are responsible for developing relationships, asking questions, and diving into their learning. Yet institutions are not off the hook. Indeed, as Estela Mara Bensimon explains, imagining that students alone are responsible for their college experiences perpetuates existing social inequities and misses the centrality of institutions, faculty, and staff in student success.[1] Colleges and universities must create relationship-rich environments and design "inescapable opportunities" for students to engage with peers, faculty, and staff. Institutional contexts vary considerably, of course, and there is no single or simple path to pursue these broad principles. However, the following commentary and examples illustrate some of the ways these principles are being enacted at colleges and universities today.

Every Student Must Experience Genuine Welcome and Deep Care

One of Vice Provost and Dean of Undergraduate Academic Affairs Ed Taylor's responsibilities is to deliver a tone-setting address to incoming students at the sprawling University of Washington, which enrolls more than forty-five thousand students. A major theme of his address is the centrality of relationships and belonging in the undergraduate experience. "What students need and want is a sense of place and a sense of belonging: Where's my place and who are my people? And part of that is the major—the discipline—but another part of that is being in a community of people who care about you and being in relationships with faculty and others who know you." Taylor's office supports a range of programs, from first-year interest groups (FIGs) to high-impact practices such as undergraduate research, to help UW undergraduates "find their people."

Belonging is a basic human need that takes on heightened importance in certain contexts, such as when joining a new community, and for certain populations, particularly those who are marginalized. Terrell Strayhorn's research illustrates that students' sense of belonging is related to and a consequence of mattering, of sensing that they are respected and cared about and that their presence and contributions make a positive difference to a particular community.[2] Regular expressions of welcome are a simple, powerful way to help all students feel a sense of belonging. Hyun-Soo Seo, an undergraduate peer mentor at the University of Michigan, finds that "success in mentoring, or in any facilitating role in higher education, comes from a deep-down place of actual caring. If you genuinely care about each and every student's success, happiness, and ability to thrive, mentoring becomes effortless and fulfilling." For all students to feel that care, they need to be reminded that they belong and that they can be successful. And this welcome cannot be expressed just during orientation week, because students' paths through higher education involve many new beginnings as each new term and course begins.[3] They need to feel welcome and to develop a sense of belonging each step along the way.

Relentless Welcome

David Scobey, of Bringing Theory to Practice, notes, "My research on adult students tells me about the need for what I call 'relentless welcome.'" The practices of deep caring and genuine welcome happen in powerful ways every day on college campuses, carried out both individually and institutionally.

More than forty years ago, Alexander Astin demonstrated that "student-faculty interaction has a stronger relationship to student satisfaction with the college experience than any other involvement variable, or, indeed, any other student or institutional characteristic."[4] More recently, Estela Mara Bensimon and others have critically analyzed the qualities of student-faculty interaction, paying particular attention to the experiences of students from groups that have historically been marginalized in higher education. Regardless of students' races or ethnicities, if students perceive faculty to be approachable, helpful, and encouraging, they are likely to be open to interactions with faculty and to thrive in college; if students perceive faculty to be remote, discouraging, or biased, they are likely to avoid interactions and to disengage from college.[5] Warm welcome and authentic connection form the essential foundation of positive student-faculty and student-staff relationships.

This principle is fundamental to Bryn Mawr College professor Joel Schlosser's rationale for scheduling individual conferences with his students: "I can't teach you if I don't know what you know and what you care about." While faculty or staff may not have the time to meet individually with every student, peers generally do, and they can be powerful voices of welcoming and belonging. At Brown University, Stacy Kastner, associate director of the writing center and writing support programs in the Sheridan Center for Teaching and Learning, explains that student writing tutors learn to ask, "'How are you doing?' in the first five minutes of every consultation session, and then to pause and listen even if it has nothing to do with the writing. Forming a relationship with somebody is just pausing in the chaos of Brown to ask, 'How are things going?'" This is a perfect example of a practice rooted in thoughtful peer training that is simple, inexpensive, scalable, and humane.

The following profiles from Nevada State College, the University of Iowa, and California State University–Dominguez Hills detail three approaches to communicate welcome, care, and belonging.

Nevada State College Library

Nevada State College, founded in 2002, is a Hispanic-serving institution of approximately four thousand students located near Las Vegas. As NSC is principally a commuter campus, one of the challenges faculty and staff grapple with is shaping a welcoming environment where students will choose to stick around after class. NSC librarians have taken on an important leadership role in meeting this challenge. Nathaniel King, director of library services, says, "We've been really inspired by thinking about the library space that will give students the experience of feeling that they belong to the campus." The library team adapted staff training practices from what at first blush might seem an unlikely model—the Four Seasons hotels—believing that hospitality available in luxury hotels in Las Vegas should also apply to NSC students. Frontline library staff training includes basics such as smiling at students, calling library visitors by name as much as possible, and being knowledgeable about library services so as to exceed students' expectations. (King proudly reports that the library has the highest student satisfaction ranking of any unit on campus.) Librarians have also paid attention to the physical environment of the library, including using plants to convey warmth and welcome, making the space as attractive as possible to reduce student stress.

The NSC librarians know that getting students into the library and comfortable using library services leads to increased academic success. Francesca Marineo, NSC instructional design librarian, points to the importance of effective library instruction in preparation for college-level research, which can be daunting for many students. NSC has integrated an online library instruction program into the First-Year Experience course. Students who complete the library program in that FYE course earn higher grades on research assignments in other courses, according to Marineo. The library staff have also found that use of the library collections is significantly related to retention, academic standing, and grade point average. These good outcomes hinge on making the library a place of "relentless welcome" on campus.

University of Iowa Hawk Talks

Greg Thompson, director of residence education at the University of Iowa, is responsible for the training and education of one of the most important front lines of welcome and support for many students—resident assistants (RAs) in campus housing. A common model for residence hall programming is a prescriptive one, requiring RAs to plan and implement a specific number of educational programs for their students each semester. But as Thompson observed, "We know peer-to-peer interaction is important right off the bat. So we moved to a model that helps RAs make authentic connections with students through informal conversations, because that's where the RAs are most skilled and comfortable—and that's when the students are most ready to learn from their RA."

Before the start of the semester, each RA is given a set of guided conversation topics titled Hawk Talks. Thompson explains, "An RA can engage the students beginning with questions like How are classes going? How are you finding the work? How are you doing with notetaking? How is college different from your high school experience? Are you staying on top of everything? If a student responds, 'You know, I'm struggling with note-taking,' the RA has resources ready to go to help."

Thompson finds that the relational and just-in-time approach of Hawk Talks is a more constructive and effective way for RAs to achieve their educational goals than required (and often resented) educational presentations of basic skills.

California State University–Dominguez Hills Male Success Alliance

Matthew Smith, interim associate vice president of student life and dean of students at California State University–Dominguez Hills, describes the qualities of relationships the university seeks to cultivate with all students: "Students want to know that you see them beyond just as a student in your class or on your campus, and that you care about them beyond just their academic success. And so that initial interaction with them in the beginning of your relationship is really important. You need to build trust and understanding."

At CSU–Dominguez Hills, as at many institutions across the country, male students of color too often do not experience that sense of belonging, trust, and welcome. To address this serious concern, and building on research that emphasizes the importance of peer support in black male success,[6] Smith helped form the Male Success Alliance (MSA), a homegrown initiative

he describes as being started with very modest resources—
"buttons and lint."

*It is important for us to have a space specifically for males because the
socialization process for males—particularly males of color and from
certain socioeconomic statuses—does not provide spaces for them to be
in community with one another in authentic ways. We are sitting
side-by-side watching games; we are competing on a field or on a court;
we are performing masculinity with one another, but we rarely have
opportunities to get together and talk about how we are truly feeling
and where we are going and what we are carrying with us on a
day-to-day basis. And those things truly impact learning and development for males of color. We are creating the space so these men can
band together, because we know they do not always experience that in
other spaces on or off campus. This space helps these men say, "I feel
valued and feel like I have a place here and that I belong."*

The Male Success Alliance complements its dedicated space
with a range of programming that includes an annual summit,
regular informal gatherings, and a mentoring program that has
MSA students working with local middle school males of color.
Research by Smith and colleagues demonstrates that the Male
Success Alliance's positive outcomes emerge from three interlocking themes related to the power of peer relationships: developing a sense of authentic brotherhood with other male students
of color, feeling accountable to these "brothers" in ways that
"build up each other," and cultivating a sense of personal responsibility for embodying and enacting change.[7]

The MSA initiative, like Hawk Talks and the efforts of librarians at Nevada State, enacts Terrell Strayhorn's charge "to create
conditions that foster belongingness among students" by demonstrating relentless welcome and genuine care.[8]

Every Student Must Be Inspired to Learn

Donna Linderman, associate vice chancellor for academic affairs for the City University of New York, oversees the ASAP program that is referenced in the first vignette of this chapter. She understands that a first step to help students be excited about learning is to encourage them to believe in their own capacities and talents:

> *Many of our students haven't necessarily tapped into the gifts and the skills they already have—their own tenacity, their own intelligence. We help them understand that they are fully capable—every single one of them—of earning their degrees. We ask, "What are the things that you've worked towards and achieved?" Whether it's being a great parent, being a productive member of your family, enjoying some subject in school that really resonated with you, or something else that helps them identify the strengths in themselves. That is essential to them being able to say and believe, "I am good at things, I can commit to things, and I can finish them."*

Being excited about learning has important implications that go far beyond success in the classroom. Indeed, a central finding of the 2014 Gallup-Purdue poll of thirty thousand college graduates is that "if an employed graduate had a professor who cared about them as a person, one who made them excited about learning, *and* had a mentor who encouraged them to pursue their dreams," that individual reported higher levels of workplace engagement and thriving in their well-being.[9]

Inspiring Learning

A wealth of knowledge exists about educational practices that can increase student motivation to learn. In *How Learning Works*, Susan Ambrose and her co-authors summarize research-based strategies to help faculty "increase the value that students place on the goals and activities that [faculty] have identified and created for them, as well as strategies to help [faculty] strengthen students' expectancies and create an environment that supports motivation."[10] These include, for example, connecting course material to students' interests, assigning authentic and real-world problems, designing student work that is appropriately challenging, and helping students set high but attainable expectations for their own work.[11]

The following institutional examples from Hope College and Brown University provide more details of relationship-rich approaches to inspire learning.

Hope College Day1 Research Communities

At Hope College, a small liberal arts college in western Michigan, Day1 research immerses first-semester students into ongoing scholarly projects alongside faculty and advanced undergraduate peers. Some Day1 communities focus on regional ecology by studying Lake Michigan or the local watershed, and others focus on lab-based science or applied engineering projects. For instance, the two dozen first-semester students who join the Phage group in Day1 take a yearlong sequence of biology courses that requires each student to sample soil to isolate a virus that infects bacteria (a phage), characterize and name the phage, and then sequence and analyze its DNA. Ford Fishman joined Phage when he started at Hope, and he now plans to go to graduate school to study computational biology: "Getting to know Dr. Best and getting in his lab right away put me on the path to where I am right now. The second semester of Phage is very computationally heavy and I found I like that stuff a lot. That semester got me interested in my career path." Fishman's Day1 experience not only shaped his long-term trajectory but also connected him with his most important mentor in college: "I've been researching with Dr. Best every other semester since then. And my relationship with him is by far my best faculty relationship I have on campus."

Many of the Day1 students also live in the same residence hall during their first year, weaving their academic and social lives together in ways that echo the scholarship on effective living-learning communities.[12] Abby Pearch, who enrolled in Phage and later decided to major in biomedical engineering, recalls how much she benefited from the integration of her courses, her research, and living in Lichty Hall alongside other Day1 students: "In Lichty, you would walk downstairs and everyone was doing homework. A lot of times people were working on the same thing and if you had a question, you could find someone who could help you answer it. I was always there, surrounded by other students who were working on science, too." This kind of environment makes learning infectious. By anchoring this experience in students' first semester, literally from day 1, this program sets students up to be highly motivated and relational learners throughout college.

Brown University Problem-Solving Fellows

The Problem-Solving Fellows Program at Brown University trains and supports undergraduates to be effective peer tutors in STEM courses. The program adapts Brown's well-established Writing Fellows[13] approach by requiring participating students to enroll in a course, The Theory and Practice of Problem Solving. Christina Smith, who directs this program and teaches the course, finds that students experience a double benefit from studying topics such as mindsets and metacognition as they prepare to be Problem-Solving Fellows; they are better prepared to be peer tutors, and they are also more confident and self-aware as students: "I regularly hear students in the course say things like, 'I wish I would have taken this course when I was a fresh-man. The things that I'm learning now are things that I wish I could have applied from my first semester at Brown.'"

The Problem-Solving Fellows' greatest impact, however, is on their peers. Not only do the fellows help students navigate chal-lenging courses, but they also support them to become more skill-ful and motivated learners. Smith notes that in group problem-solving activities in STEM courses, the fellows circulate among student groups, offering encouragement and suggestions but never solving problems for their peers. These passing interactions often have a tangible effect on the energy and focus of a group. Fellows also work with peers one-on-one outside of class. In those situa-tions, Smith explains, the fellow may find that "the student says they are perplexed by the questions, but then the fellow realizes, Oh, this student has a fixed mindset about X or Y. And when that happens, the fellow will work to help the student cultivate a growth mindset, rather than directly focusing on the questions."

The relationships created by Problem-Solving Fellows with students in and out of the classroom, like the Day1 Research Communities, can be educationally powerful and inspiring.

Every Student Must Develop a Web of Significant Relationships

More than thirty years ago, Vincent Tinto, in his pioneering re-search on student departure from college, referenced the "intricate web of reciprocal relationships which binds students to the com-munal life of the institution."[14] More recently, Roberta Espinoza has studied the "pivotal moments" in the education of low-income Latinx students, revealing that "academic success is hardly an indi-vidual affair but rather is the result of the formal and informal aca-demic interventions of educators who foster meaningful relation-ships with students to transform their educational trajectories."[15] Echoing Espinoza, Brad Johnson uses the term *mentoring constella-*

tions to describe the web of relationships that students form with people on campus who take active interest in and actions to advance those students' learning, professional development, and personal well-being. Further, he suggests that a "mentoring constellation will be strongest and most effective when the [student] is intentional about forming the constellation and when the constellation contains good diversity."[16] This proposition is reinforced by Janice McCabe's research about the in-college and long-term importance of the nature of students' friendship networks as undergraduates. The most resilient and positive peer networks in college, she finds, are characterized by students who share "academic multiplex ties" that involve mutual emotional support, instrumental assistance, and intellectual engagement.[17]

Weaving Webs

Whether we describe the concept as a cluster or a constellation or a web of relationships, the point remains the same: over time, one of the most important things students can do in college is build a diverse community of advisors, coaches, mentors, teachers, friends, and confidants to look to for inspiration, information, challenge, direction, and opportunities—the people who give the gifts of listening and helping students to see in themselves what they alone cannot see. Johnson's research on these webs of relationships in a variety of settings demonstrates, as he told us:

> *Those of us who have mentors just do better. It doesn't matter whether you're looking at higher education, the military, or corporate America, those of us who have mentors get more opportunities. We have broader networks. We make more money. We get more promotions. We report later on that we're happier with both our career and our lives. We tend to feel more comfortable balancing work and professional obligations. For all of these reasons, the benefits of mentoring really are not even in question anymore.*

A 2018 national poll of four thousand college graduates with bachelor's degrees captured the impact of webs of undergraduate relationships with mentors and other influential people in students' lives.[18] The poll found that alumni who reported having had from seven to ten significant relationships with faculty and staff were more than three times as likely to report their college experience as "very rewarding" as compared to graduates with no such relationships. Even a small number of important relationships matter; alumni with just one or two significant relationships were twice as likely to rate college as "very rewarding" as compared to graduates with no such relationships. The poll also found that students typically start building their mentoring constellations early in their undergraduate careers. Sixty percent reported meeting their most influential faculty or staff member in college during their first year, and 79 percent formed their most significant peer relationship during that year. Students usually meet these influential faculty and peers in their courses, meaning that the classroom experience, and particularly the first-year classroom experience, is pivotal. Finally, the poll uncovered a disturbing gap: first-generation college students were more likely to report having zero influential relationships (15 percent) than those with a college-educated parent (6 percent). And while 29 percent of students with a college-educated parent reported seven or more significant relationships with faculty or staff, this was true for only 17 percent of first-generation students.[19]

These data underscore the importance of institutions taking responsibility for helping students to weave their webs of significant relationships in college. Faculty and staff must "intervene" (to borrow Espinoza's term) to support and challenge students to learn how to build meaningful connections with peers, faculty, staff, and others on and beyond campus. The following examples from Nevada State College and the University of Michigan provide illustrations of how two very different institutions are doing just that.

Nevada State College Nepantla Program

The Nepantla Program at Nevada State College is named for a Nahuatl word meaning "in between—a space of change and transition," which acknowledges the personal, academic, and cultural change experienced by program participants. Nepantla serves first-generation college students, nearly all of whom are Latinx and many of whom have deeply rooted cultural traditions that emphasize the centrality of family and the importance of hard work, persistence, and self-reliance.[20] These students regularly experience what Gloria Anzaldúa has called "un choque,"[21] a cultural collision, as they move back and forth between their home communities and the academy. Even as they navigate this "in between," many Nepantla students commute long distances and hold down one or more jobs while attending college full time; some face additional challenges including food or housing insecurity and family members struggling with immigration status.

According to Nepantla's director, Leilani Carreño, the program is rooted in a combination of high expectations of student success and a wide web of advisors, mentors, faculty, staff, and peers: "We expect that once you are in this program, you will be a part of this community and you will have mentorship from the day you arrive through your date of graduation." Nepantla students begin with a relationship-rich summer bridge program that helps them make the academic and social transition into their first semester on campus while also building a strong sense of belonging and peer support within the group.[22] Many students enroll in cohort-based classes designed for Nepantla students, such as Professor Leila Pazargadi's introductory English course, where a narrative approach is used to encourage students to write about their own college journeys, further reinforcing that sense of belonging in college. Students are also supported by well-trained peer mentors and have ready access to counseling and other services. Nepantla supplements these offerings with a strong program of parental education that helps family members understand the demands of college life and encourages both students and parents to balance expectations related to school, work, and home.

Each of these overlapping aspects of Nepantla is designed to help students build webs of meaningful relationships. As Carreño emphasizes, "It's important that a first-generation college student has a community—their tribe, per se—that will support them through their college education." Nepantla is based on respect for the cultural wealth that students bring to campus from their families and home communities; at the same time, it recognizes that students will need peer mentoring and relationship-rich experiences with faculty and staff as they navigate that space "in between" at Nevada State College.

University of Michigan Mentoring Consortium

Ayeza Siddiqi arrived at the University of Michigan as an international, first-generation, transfer student. Of her early days on campus she says, "I had no idea what I was doing. Navigating such a large, decentralized university was really difficult, and I often felt like the university wasn't designed for people who look like me." Fortunately, she had signed up for Transfer Connections, a program that matches new transfer students with more experienced and extensively trained peers who help them gain confidence, make connections, and build academic skills. Siddiqi benefited so much from the program that she decided to give back, becoming a Transfer Connections peer mentor and then, after graduating from Michigan and earning a graduate degree at another institution, being hired to direct the program.

Siddiqi also leads the Mentoring Consortium, an initiative that brings together practitioners from the dozens of undergraduate mentoring programs that exist across the university. The consortium aims to ameliorate a problem many students encounter at large institutions like Michigan: the wealth of opportunities can overwhelm students. As one student recently asked, "As a gay transfer student who is also a military veteran, which peer mentoring program is right for me?" The answer to that question, of course, is not simple and should not be determined by the first program the student happens to encounter. Instead, that student needs to be able to talk with a knowledgeable and skillful person who can help them think through their goals and needs and then make an informed choice about which program, if any, is right for them.

The Mentoring Consortium informs staff from dozens of different programs about the array of options available to students and allows them to make personal connections with one another so they can provide both warm welcome and practical guidance to the students who bring them questions and concerns. As Siddiqi explains, "Sometimes colleagues in different programs will recommend a student come talk with me because, as a practicing Muslim woman on campus, I can offer them a particular kind of advice and support. Those students ordinarily wouldn't find me because they aren't in Transfer Connections, but we can better help all our students by knowing and trusting our colleagues across campus."

By building networks of connection among student life and academic staff at the University of Michigan, the Mentoring Consortium, like Nepantla, supports undergraduates in developing their own webs of relationships.

Every Student Must Explore Questions of Meaning and Purpose

Being the first person in her family to graduate from high school or attend college, Adriana Aldana felt proud of her ability to succeed in her education without help from others: "I vividly remember having to advocate for myself every step of the way. I believed that my achievement in school was my responsibility and no one else's." Even while working full time, she excelled in her studies at

California State University, Northridge, but, she says, for "the first three years of college I wandered aimlessly taking courses with no long-term goal in mind." During her third year, an academic advisor explained that she was on track to graduate with a degree in Chicano Studies and Psychology, so she decided to do that, but still did not feel she had a sense of direction.

In the campus food court one day during her junior year, Aldana heard high-achieving classmates talking about applying to graduate school, and she noticed that many of the people whom she admired in the community had earned advanced degrees. Intrigued, she sat down at a computer and "Thanks to Google, I quickly learned about graduate school and my urgent need for research experience." She thought about her options and then one day in the fall of 2005:

> I waited patiently for all the students in my developmental psychology course to trickle out of class to ask Dr. Chavira about joining her research lab. I was nervous since I had only known her for a couple of weeks and this was the first time I had spoken to her outside of class. Would she deny my request? Anxiously, I approached her and inquired about joining her research team. I could see her hesitancy. She said that she typically did not invite students to participate in her lab if she had no prior experience with them. Nevertheless, she warmly suggested I attend her next lab meeting, and we would go from there.

After being accepted, Aldana found a sense of purpose in Professor Chavira's lab. She no longer "wandered aimlessly" (albeit very successfully) through college; instead, she experienced a "pivotal moment"[23] of meaning and mentoring that set her on a path toward her life's work. After earning a PhD in social work and developmental psychology from the University of Michigan, Aldana became an assistant professor of social work at CSU–Dominguez Hills, teaching students (many of them with educational histories like her own) to think critically about their communities and identities.

While Aldana's story has a successful ending, it has elements of tenuousness as well. Like many of the first-generation students we interviewed, she developed a sense of purpose in her education almost by chance. What if she had not heard the conversation in the food court about graduate school? What if she had not summoned the courage to pursue an undergraduate research mentor? What if Professor Chavira had not welcomed this unfamiliar student into her lab? Aldana's story frames the larger issue of why asking students the big questions of meaning and purpose should not be left to happenstance.

Lack of engagement with questions of meaning and purpose is a problem that applies to students across the socioeconomic spectrum, including well-to-do students who have ridden a metaphorical conveyor belt to college without giving much thought to what they expect from higher education or themselves. Sharon Parks is among the most astute commentators of our time about engaging college students with questions of meaning and purpose. In her book *Big Questions, Worthy Dreams*, she references a panel of undergraduates who were asked about when and where they discuss the guiding questions of their lives. One student responded, "We are numb to those issues." Parks went on to observe, "Further discussion reveals that this is not exactly a consequence of either apathy or skepticism but rather a lifestyle that has no room for such questions."[24] She goes on to underscore the importance of critical thinking, the bedrock of the liberal arts tradition: "It has always been the case that some students, seemingly motivated only by utilitarian concerns, simply never consider or abandon the hope of finding meaning and purpose that is truly satisfying. They need initiation into critical thought, in part so that they may reflect on the careerism to which they have become subject."[25]

Adding to the problem are perfunctory, transactional advising systems that reduce students' chances of getting to the big questions. Richard Light notes that "those who simply use the opportunity to get a quick signature on a study card are missing out on conversations that would change their perspective on what they are studying, why they are studying it, and how what they study fits into a bigger picture of their lives, and what new ideas might be worth considering."[26]

Big Questions

If higher education is to fulfill its purposes, every student must be challenged to encounter big questions such as these, as well as another that Vice Provost Randy Bass at Georgetown University suggests every student must consider: "Institutions should be places that ask all students, 'Who are you becoming for other people, not just for yourself?'" This, indeed, is a big question every student should grapple with in college (and throughout life), from the large numbers of students trying to escape poverty to the privileged few with trust funds.

The following examples from LaGuardia Community College and the University of Washington illustrate some of the ways these two different institutions invite students to consider questions of meaning, purpose, and identity.

LaGuardia Community College First-Year Programs

Associate Provost Bret Eynon describes LaGuardia Community College students as "first generation times two. They are not only the first in their families coming to college, they are also overwhelmingly immigrants and second-language learners. Helping these students form important relationships in college is a key piece of helping them make the transition to becoming college students, New Yorkers, and Americans."

How does an institution like LaGuardia take on the audacious challenge of asking all its students to examine the big questions of meaning and purpose, especially when many students' most urgent priorities are to get a higher-paying job, improve their English language proficiency, and provide for their families? The answer lies in LaGuardia's integrative and comprehensive approach to education—LaGuardia's peer mentoring programs are for all students, not only for students in the ASAP program described earlier in this chapter. As Eynon explains, "All of us (faculty, staff, and administrative leadership) build students' lives into the center of what we are doing—building it into our pedagogy, building it into our curriculum, building it into campus employment and other out-of-class opportunities, and finding ways to help students make connections between their college lives and the rest of their lives."

The heart of this approach is the e-portfolio that students develop as they progress through the curriculum at LaGuardia. Each student's e-portfolio is centered on two core questions: "Who am I?" and "Who am I becoming?" Students consider these questions in their courses, with peer mentors both in and out of the classroom, and throughout the high-touch advising process. Although LaGuardia uses a common platform for students to document their evolving responses to these big questions, both the educational process and the portfolio are designed to flexibly meet students where they are in their lives, help them make linkages between their studies and every other dimension of their lives, and ensure that big questions guide their thinking and planning throughout college.[27] The portfolios are a powerful tool on their own, and they also enable mentoring conversations to happen routinely throughout the college because faculty, staff, and peers know that every student is regularly being asked to reflect on "Who am I?" and "Who am I becoming?"

This is precisely what William Sullivan means when he calls for "a new attention to the exploration of large, orienting questions about the world and human identity, about meaning and life purpose, all of which have been central concerns of the tradition of liberal education."[28] LaGuardia is reinventing this idea for the new majority student. That LaGuardia students are guided along the way by supportive and trained peers who have already walked this path ahead of them adds a special element of authenticity to their approach (more on LaGuardia's peer mentoring programs in chapter 5).

The desire for a good job and a better life for one's family and the examination of the bigger questions about what gives life meaning and purpose are not mutually exclusive pursuits. Of course students should be concerned with both. The quality of relationships that students form with faculty, advisors, mentors, and peers will make this integrative thinking possible—and potentially transformative.

University of Washington Undergraduate Research

Undergraduate research is among the relationship-rich academic experiences with the most powerful outcomes for all students. Undergraduate research programs immerse students in relationship-rich environments that typically include mentors or supervisors for individual research and a broader mentoring community of peers, professors, and other scholars who are pursuing similar lines of inquiry.[29] But a gap exists between the promise and practice of these programs. Those engaged in undergraduate research disproportionately are "economically advantaged students with family legacies of higher education," even though participation in this form of mentored research is particularly beneficial for students from historically underserved groups.[30]

When Samantha Paskvan left home in Alaska to enroll at the University of Washington, she had planned to study chemistry and pursue her passion for dance. She quickly found a family in the dance program, but she aspired to a career in chemistry, so she decided to seek out an undergraduate research experience in that department: "I kept waiting for the class or the teacher that would spark my interest so I could jump on their research project." To her surprise, she found that professor in a genetics course. After the term ended, she nervously told the professor of her interest in undergraduate research and was invited for an interview: "I brought in my résumé and we talked about all of the different projects that they were doing in the lab and also all about me. It was incredibly invigorating to be able to talk about science, research, and life." She joined the lab and quickly found support from "the whole lab community" of other undergrads, grad students, postdocs, and faculty: "I wasn't just a pair of hands in the lab, we were constantly talking about the science behind everything." Paskvan soon spent eighteen hours each week doing research because she found the science so stimulating and also because she enjoyed the "validating" community of this "female-dominated lab": "Beyond the serious science we're doing, there's this whole other aspect of caring about each other's lives. The faculty will make the time to ask, How are your classes going? What are you thinking about for next year? What are you getting involved in outside of the lab? Who do you want to be after you graduate? And then they would really listen and encourage me, even when I wasn't sure if I knew what I was doing or where I was going."

In her undergraduate research lab, Paskvan experienced a profound and reinforcing combination of welcome, learning, relationships, and purpose. Faculty created the conditions for that mentoring community by motivating students to work hard and cultivating students' sense of belonging in science and in the lab. Like the portfolio project at LaGuardia Community College, an undergraduate research lab at the University of Washington became fertile ground for deeply meaningful learning.

* * *

When Asma Shauib enrolled at LaGuardia Community College, she barely spoke English and she had no experience with higher education. She failed all of her placement exams so, discouraged, she enrolled in the CUNY Language Immersion Program (CLIP):

> This program changed my life and my whole idea of education. When I first started taking classes there, I thought it would just be reading and writing and speaking in English. That's it. But the faculty at CLIP believed in me more than I did in myself. They asked me to share my thoughts and my ideas, my goals, my dreams of what I wanted to be, what I wanted to achieve. I did that, but deep inside me, I did not think that any of that was possible, especially for someone from my background and culture. But they told me that those are great ideas and we can see you achieving them. They said I'm a "shining star." When they first said that to me, I thought, "No one has ever told me that." So when they told me that, I decided, okay, I'm going to work for it and I'm going to work hard. I stayed with the CLIP program for a whole year. Now that I've finished CLIP, I still go back and visit them and they still tell me that I'm a shining star. They see that in me, and I keep that in mind whenever I'm stressed out or think that I will not make it.

Relationship-rich undergraduate education, like what Asma Shauib experienced at CLIP and what other students experienced in other programs profiled in this chapter, is rooted in relentless welcome, inspired learning, webs of relationships, and meaningful questions. These four guiding principles help students develop new visions of themselves as people who are capable, who belong in higher education, and who can make a difference in their communities and in the world.

Acting on these principles is difficult for individuals and for institutions. The next chapter considers why this work is so hard.

Chapter Two

Why Is This So Hard?

I don't know about you, but in my graduate training the word teaching never came up. Much less pedagogy. Much less student learning. Those words were not part of the conversation in any way.

—Bret Eynon, LaGuardia Community College

To explain why building and sustaining relationship-rich environments can be so hard, this chapter explores some of the primary challenges in these endeavors—some pertaining to people and others to institutions. To be certain, these are significant barriers. Identifying and analyzing them honestly and systemically, however, is a major step toward creating change. Later chapters in this book provide examples of people who have worked through or even largely dismantled these barriers. First, though, a voice from our research:

David Latimer is a fourth-generation college graduate who believes in the power of education to transform lives. For the past five years he has worked with students in the Accelerated Study in Associate Programs (ASAP) at City Tech, part of the City University of New York system. Latimer has been an advisor and mentor for many hundred low-income students as they begin or restart their college careers. Over thousands of hours of conversations with these students, he has heard one overriding theme:

Students fear failure and being challenged beyond their limits. They may not have been challenged academically in high school and for the first time are really experiencing academic rigor. They fear embarrassing their families—being afraid to come home and say, "I am not achieving in college right now. I'm struggling." They fear talking to a professor because a professor represents an intimidating authority figure. They are not sure how to approach them. They also resist asking for help or asking for a tutor, because utilizing a tutor is perceived as not being smart. They do not want to go to counseling when they have emotional problems, because that's for people who are weak. The fear of shame is everywhere.

In our interviews at colleges and universities across the country, we heard Latimer's words echoed by students, faculty, and staff. Imposter syndrome and shame make it hard for students to make connections with and seek help from peers, faculty, and staff. Some groups of students face particularly high hurdles erected by social inequities, but none are immune. Indeed, many faculty and staff report these same feelings of inadequacy as they struggle to teach, advise, and mentor students. The institutional structures and reward systems of many colleges and universities create additional distance between students and the institution's faculty and staff. Rapid demographic changes among students—and, more slowly, among staff and faculty—further challenge the structures and assumptions that undergird many higher education institutions.

Individual and Situational Factors: Isolation and Imposter Syndrome

At every institution we visited, students described feeling like imposters.[1] A student at a highly selective liberal arts college recounted "being mortified by my own seeming deficits and by feeling paralyzed by comparison and insecurity." A community college student introduced herself by saying, "I come from an academically challenged background. I wasn't the best student in high school, so I just assumed I wasn't smart enough or bright enough for college." The educational and personal backgrounds of these two students could hardly be more different, yet they, like so many of their peers, expressed deep doubts about their own capacity to be successful academically and to belong in higher education.

These feelings are compounded by explicit or implicit cues in the academic environment that encourage students to see college as an individualistic, anxiety-inducing slog. Claude Steele has coined the term *stereotype threat* to describe how a person's performance is affected by "identity contingencies—the things you have to deal with in a situation because you have a given social identity, because you are old, young, gay, a white male, a woman, black, Latino, politically conservative or liberal, diagnosed with bipolar disorder, a cancer patient, and so on."[2] Research on stereotype threat makes plain that outcomes (a student drops out of a chemistry course) that at first might seem to be attributable to individual behavior often are significantly influenced by social and situational factors (she is the only female student in a course taught by a male professor and in labs supervised by male teaching assistants). Neither social identities nor situational factors *determine* negative outcomes, but both can powerfully shape a student's experiences in college. The good news is that Steele's research demonstrates effective ways to counter stereotype threat in education: "Establishing trust through demanding but supportive relationships, fostering hopeful narratives about belonging in the setting, arranging informal cross-group conversations to reveal that identity is not the sole cause of one's negative experiences in the setting, representing critical abilities as learnable, and using [student]-centered teaching techniques."[3]

Unfortunately, this research has not been systematically put into practice in higher education. For instance, students on one campus told us about their general chemistry professor who asked his 650 students on the first day of class, "How many of you are pre-med?" When several hundred students raised their hands, he commented, "Well, we will get that number down." Much more often than such bold pronouncements of doom, students reported encountering everyday doubts and discouragement seeded by the academic environment. A student at a research university told us that in many of his classes "the professor just throws information at you, hoping something sticks, and then you go home and teach yourself." Even in small classes, such as writing courses, many students experience high levels of stress and doubt. Rachel Herzl-Betz, assistant director of the Writing Center at Nevada State College, explained that "a lot of students come in believing writing is very important but that they are bad writers. It's absolutely heartbreaking to see some students who have wonderful ideas and care deeply about self-expression but who feel that because they didn't score X on this standardized test that they are just not good at it." Eileen Kogl Camfield documented similar student experiences in an introductory college writing course, quoting one student, Tara, who stated, "Writing felt like going on a long scary rollercoaster with the Grinch anxiously waiting on the other side to judge me."[4]

Students respond to these pressures in a variety of ways. Alexa Oleson at the University of Iowa described her strategy as a first-year student: "I was super shy when I first came to campus. I would go to class, sit down, and look as unwelcoming as possible. I didn't want anyone to sit next to me." Another student, Rojan K C at LaGuardia Community College, felt lost: "I'm an international student. It's completely a different environment here from the perspective of culture and learning. At first, I was really confused. I didn't know whom to ask for what kind of help because the college is so huge."

Indeed, many students seem *not* to look to anyone else—a peer, an instructor, a staff member—for any kind of assistance. Maruth Figueroa directs the Learning Center at California State

University–Dominguez Hills, one of the most ethnically diverse universities in the United States. She underscored the research on low-income college students nationally as she told us: "When we look at our student population at Dominguez, and specifically when we looked at underserved students, help-seeking behavior is not something that comes easy, or it's not something that they do." Yet we heard a similar message from a student life administrator at the University of Michigan, a predominantly white and highly selective institution: "The general student perception here is that asking for help is not what you want to do." This message echoed across every institution we visited; many students of all backgrounds are hesitant to ask for help, and institutional environments often reinforce this tendency to believe that college is a solo endeavor. Students are ashamed to admit what they do not know and are embarrassed to let others know that they are confused or uncertain or struggling with a personal issue. Administrators at Georgia State University saw this dynamic in action when they created an artificial intelligence–based chatbot that could respond quickly to questions students submitted via text. Timothy Renick, senior vice president for student success at GSU, notes that many students *prefer* to ask questions of the chatbot because they know that no one will be judging them. The fear of being seen as an imposter runs deep.

Although isolation, shame, and imposter syndrome are common among college students, these feelings are not necessarily evenly distributed, nor are all identity contingencies equivalent. Our students are products of educational, cultural, and economic systems that are highly inequitable, preparing them differently for the demands of higher education and perpetuating stereotypes of who is or is not likely to succeed in college. For instance, the racial-ethnic achievement gap in US higher education is well documented, but research also demonstrates sharp psychosocial disparities between white and black students, including more "belonging uncertainty" and more pervasive feelings of imposterism among black undergraduates.[5] These feelings affect individuals differently, because the experiences, assets, and capacities within any group of students are not monolithic,[6] and institutional and social contexts also matter.[7] Yet some students do come to higher education with stronger senses of belonging and more educational capital than their peers, while others arrive in college with profound uncertainty about whether they belong—and institutional, social, and other factors may implicitly cue or explicitly reinforce those doubts. For instance, Bryn Mawr student Khadijah Seay recalled:

> Coming to college was a difficult experience for me. There was the just being away from home part. And then there was race. I never felt like I was a student first. I was always black first, and then a student. For example, during my junior year, I remember walking into class on the day after Tamir Rice was killed by police. I was distraught. I walked into class and sat there, and it seemed like no one else was fazed by it. The day went on as usual for other students, but I didn't go to my other three classes that day. It was just so surreal to have all of this weight on me because of something that happened and not feeling that reflected at all by the students and professors around me.

Seay's experience was by no means unique. Black students all over the nation, including on our own campus, have had similar painful experiences following instances of racial violence that plague our country. And, too often, faculty, staff, and institutions let these students down when we leave them completely on their own to process grief, anger, and disbelief. Former president of Bates College Donald Harward reminds us that too many of our campuses have yet to master a "grammar of compassion." We must take this idea to heart and step up when tragedies and traumas affect our students. "Because the importance of the undergraduate experience is one of being heard," according to Harward, "and in being heard, students discover they have a voice and that the voice is valued."

In another example of outside events sparking deeper doubts about belonging, Liz Stevenson, an ASAP advisor at City Tech in New York, told us about a student who is part of the federal Deferred Action for Childhood Arrivals (DACA) program coming to her the day after the 2016 presidential election to ask if he still could attend school, telling her, "Maybe I'm not allowed to be in college anymore. Maybe I'm supposed to drop out now." Fortunately, Stevenson was able to immediately assure this student of her own and City Tech's commitment to his education; she also worked with colleagues to quickly share that message more broadly with the college's students, knowing that not everyone has a trusted advisor to talk with about topics like DACA.

Still other students do not feel confident in their understanding of the rules of the game in higher education. One advisor reported that an advisee almost withdrew from a first-semester writing course because she was afraid to ask "stupid" questions about academic terminology she did not understand. Other students explained that they only discovered by accident the positive benefits of being in a calculus study group or effective ways to approach a faculty member outside of class with a question. Because they have become higher education insiders, faculty and staff often do not even notice their own implicit assumptions or use of jargon. As Anthony Jack has observed, "When professors mention office hours, often only on the first day of classes, they tell students *when* office hours are. They almost never say *what* they are."[8]

Some of the concerns we heard may seem like minor issues, but when students already feel ashamed and wonder if they are imposters, even small misunderstandings and tacit cues can reinforce the internal narrative that "I don't know what I'm doing" and "I don't belong here." Research on shame demonstrates that such doubts can quickly produce a form of learned helplessness, convincing students that they are bound to fail before they even begin.[9] Imposter syndrome also has troubling correlations with anxiety, depression, and psychological distress among undergraduates.[10] In short, students who experience college as a place and time of fear and shame are less likely than their peers to build the kinds of student–student, and student–faculty, and student–staff relationships that nurture belonging, success, and well-being.

Many of these same feelings can be found among faculty and staff across higher education. Mary Deane Sorcinelli, who has worked with dozens of research universities to develop programs to support early career faculty, told us that "on issues of imposter syndrome and isolation and need for community, you could talk about a parallel between some of the entering students we have and some of the entering faculty we have." Scholars who study faculty and staff careers cast an even wider net: "The current work environment in higher education and personality traits of those attracted to it align rather closely to those factors that contribute to the development of imposter tendencies."[11] These general pressures can be initiated or reinforced by personal, situational, and institutional factors. For example, research demonstrates that belonging uncertainty often is experienced by faculty of color at predominantly white institutions and by women in male-dominated disciplines, and also by adjunct faculty in general.[12] As with students, faculty and staff who feel like imposters or who have doubts about belonging are less likely than their peers to seek help and to build relationships with students or colleagues.[13] Isolation begets isolation.

Later in the book we will explore research-based approaches individuals and institutions can use to counter these negative beliefs and to encourage all students, faculty, and staff to feel that they belong, to be more resilient, and to adopt help-seeking behaviors. For now, however, we emphasize that feelings of doubt, fear, and shame are pervasive among college students; that stereotype threat and situational factors often contribute significantly to outcomes; and that students who feel like imposters or who doubt they belong are unlikely to take the kinds of steps necessary to build relationships that will help them to succeed. These factors might seem to make success impossible for some situations and for some groups of students, but Rebecca Cox's studies of community college students lead her to a powerful and counterintuitive charge: "Rather than ask why and how so many college students meet with failure, perhaps it is more useful to consider how students persist in the face of such powerful urges to quit."[14]

Institutional Challenges: Classrooms, Curricula, and Reward Systems

Entrenched structures in American higher education work against relationship-rich undergraduate education. First, some classrooms do not engage students meaningfully in learning or in the human connections that seed motivation, sometimes because our institutions have not invested adequately in the faculty or their professional development. Second, pathways through the curricula can be uninspired and isolating, leaving students alone to drift through college. Third, and perhaps most significant, institutional reward systems often do not value relational teaching or interactions with students outside of the classroom; in fact, faculty and staff at some institutions mentor students at their own professional peril.

Classrooms That Are Not Relational

The classroom is the fundamental place of both learning and relationships in college. Vincent Tinto neatly summarized the research—and the challenge—more than two decades ago: "The college classroom lies at the center of the educational activity structure of institutions of higher education. . . . Indeed, for students who commute to college, especially those who have multiple obligations outside of college, the classroom may be the only place where students and faculty meet, where education in the formal sense is experienced. For those students, in particular, the classroom is the crossroads where the social and academic meet."[15]

Too often, classrooms are *not* rich sites of learning and connection. In 2018 an observational study of STEM classes taught by 548 individual faculty at twenty-five North American universities documented the teaching practices undergraduates experienced in 709 different courses, ranging from large introductory sections to small upper-level classes. Only 18 percent of the observed classes employed "student-centered" pedagogies such as structured active learning activities integrated throughout a lecture; by contrast, 55 percent of the observations revealed didactic teaching that included limited or no "observed student involvement except sporadic questions from and to the students."[16] In this kind of classroom environment, students are unlikely to develop the meaningful relationships with peers or faculty that would help them learn and persist in college.

Many introductory courses are taught by contingent faculty who, no matter their dedication and pedagogical capacity, have little opportunity to build lasting relationships with their students. And when full-time faculty teach these courses, the class size or the number of sections taught can create a difficult "arithmetic of engagement."[17] Megan Klein, who teaches sociology and anthropology at Oakton Community College, pointed out that if you are teaching five or more sections in a semester (sometimes, in her experience, up to nine in one term!), and each section has thirty-five students, building meaningful relationships with students—or even getting to know all of their names—can feel like an insurmountable task.

Many faculty also feel unprepared to teach or poorly equipped to change the way they teach.[18] Matt Reed, a community college dean and columnist for *Inside Higher Ed*, described his own experience: "The sum total of my pedagogical training before TA-ing in my first class consisted of the professor saying, 'You'll be fine.'"[19] Despite that reality for some in higher education, more and more faculty and graduate students are working to improve their teaching and to meet the needs of their students. Research clearly demonstrates the effectiveness of educational development programs to support learning about teaching, course design, equity, and assessment.[20]

Curriculum That Does Not Connect

The undergraduate curriculum often creates a further barrier to making classes relationship-rich experiences. Vice Provost Randy Bass of Georgetown told us:

> *The general pattern of students is that they have a relatively homogenous, relatively unsatisfying set of academic engagements until, at best, they get into their upper division and major courses and then find that special relationship with that "one person." I think we need far greater variety of learning contexts in the first two years intentionally designed for heterogeneity of engagements that would start to produce very different kinds of relationships and give faculty and students a much greater variety of interactions. This could be, for example, a short course, a project-based mentorship where every single faculty member in the department would engage with first-year students in some form.*

Indeed, at four-year institutions, the first two years tend to focus on courses, often taught in huge, impersonal lecture halls, that introduce students to disciplines and to the breadth of human knowledge. This curricular design may have intellectual merit as a way to establish a firm foundation for in-depth study later in college, but research suggests that many students are adrift and isolated in this sea of general education.[21] Introductory courses need to be reconceived to emphasize relationships:

having our best teachers interacting with students; creating intellectually stimulating active learning courses, including community-based experiences and course-based undergraduate research opportunities that require students to work with peers and others on purposeful projects; and helping students identify potential mentors much earlier in their undergraduate careers.

While many institutions have adopted first-year seminars in an effort to work against the tide, too often these well-intentioned programs either fail to meet their full potential or leave students with just one relationship-rich experience in their first two years of college.[22]

Reward Systems That Do Not Value Relationships

Brad Johnson speaks with pride about a program at the United States Naval Academy, where he teaches, that enrolls some six hundred undergraduate midshipmen each year in a National Outdoor Leadership School (NOLS) experience. Accompanied by faculty and NOLS staff, the midshipmen travel to a glacier in Alaska or to the Wind River Canyon in Wyoming to do high-altitude mountaineering in small teams: "I hear from midshipmen that these very intensive moments are some of the most important in their entire time at the Naval Academy in terms of bonding with faculty who are assuming the immediate first-person role-modeling leadership in extremis."

Despite the high value of this type of role modeling, Johnson notes a paradox for most colleges and universities: "When you get to that promotion and tenure moment, very few people are asking you about mentoring." For institutions that are serious about preparing leaders (as almost all higher education institutions purport to do), Johnson offers clear guidance about making relationships count: "Administrative and faculty leaders must make it clear that mentoring is part of our identity. It's what we do. We must put our money where our mouth is in rewarding faculty who are doing well in devoting time to these educational relationships."

And yet, rewards for mentoring or advising students are not even on the table on many campuses, as one faculty member at a prestigious research university told us: "There is such an emphasis on research that I feel the interpersonal relationships with students aren't valued." That leaves faculty like Assistant Professor of Astronomy Emily Rauscher at the University of Michigan having to make intentional and personal choices to dedicate time to undergraduate research students: "When I think about how I invest my bucket of time throughout the year across the many different things that I have to or want to be involved with, I'm okay with some fraction of my time being useless in terms of advancing my career because mentoring these undergraduates accomplishes other goals I have for myself."

This issue reaches far beyond research universities, however. Cathy Davidson captures the problem in her book *The New Education*: "Even if professors are actually teaching a lot and spending a good portion of their time in that effort, the overall ecosystem of higher education does not reward good teaching in the same way it rewards (and requires) measurable 'outputs'—peer-reviewed articles, books, professional papers, and grants."[23]

Compounding the faculty reward–related problems are inadequate measures to evaluate the effectiveness of teaching, mentoring, advising, and other educational relationships. A faculty member at an institution that is deeply committed to student-centered teaching told us about a colleague who was denied tenure, even though in his opinion the colleague "was our finest teacher. The problem was our student ratings don't capture student learning or relationship-building, and in our review system those ratings are the most important factor." At another institution, a group of committed undergraduate research mentors lamented the difficulty of capturing the outcomes of their work with students. Some undergraduate researchers present their scholarly work at professional conferences or are admitted to prestigious graduate programs, but research mentors also help some students wrestle with the realization that they do not *want* to pursue careers in their disciplines. One of those two outcomes tends to be celebrated institutionally, but each can be a mark of excellent mentoring. And undergraduate research is better understood and evaluated than much of the often invisible relationship-rich teaching, mentoring, and advising that happens on campuses; for faculty and staff of color whom students come to seeking a sense of belonging and academic support on our campuses, this relational work too often happens at the expense of their own professional advancement.[24] Unfortunately, most campuses evaluate and reward faculty teaching and mentoring, and often also the work of staff in student life, in ways that are too blunt to capture the relational nature of these activities. Indeed, scholars have demonstrated that faculty who spend more time on teaching than research are paid and promoted on average less than their peers and that evaluation and reward factors have a powerful impact on institutional culture and individual behavior.[25]

Relationship Building Is Hard but Possible

Individual and institutional barriers to relationship-rich educational experiences and environments are significant but not insurmountable. And, despite the height of the hurdles, colleges and universities have assets in this work that can be leveraged.

As a first step, we need to adopt a mindset that students bring to college assets to be developed rather than liabilities and deficits to be ameliorated—and that institutions, faculty, and staff are responsible for challenging and supporting students to learn.[26] Every institution has students with the capacities and aspirations they need to be successful in higher education. Sometimes that potential is unrecognized and unrealized, but it is there and we should not underestimate its power.

Gigi Gaultier, a senior studying aquatic and fishery sciences at the University of Washington, illustrates the mixture of capacity and doubt that many students experience in college. When she applied to the university, she was wait-listed—and devastated. But, as she related, "I was lucky enough to have a really great family and support system, and they pushed me to appeal my wait-list. My first appeal was rejected, and I thought, 'Well, they really don't want me.' But I kept pushing, and I did well in my senior courses. I'll be honest; I think just the fact that my face and my name kept on showing up again and again in admissions made someone realize, 'Okay, if we just let her in, she will stop bothering us.'"

After Gaultier received her acceptance, she eagerly registered for classes and secured a dorm room:

> But when I actually got to campus, I kept thinking that as a wait-listed student I'm probably on the lower end academically here. Sitting in these large classrooms—Chemistry 142 had 500 people or so—I convinced myself that they're all more successful than me. I was comparing myself to others and imagining all of their accomplishments. I was freaking out about a lot of things at first. It took me a full year before I decided to go to UW's Friday Harbor Labs my sophomore year to do marine biology research. That gave me a lot of hands-on applicable knowledge in my field, and also the experience of being in a small community where I felt connected with my peers and professors. When I came back to this huge campus, I started applying for opportunities to re-create that small group feel—so I've been a Freshman Interest Group leader and an orientation leader, and I've completed a Husky Leadership Certificate. That's where I've found my place and developed my confidence here.

Not all students have the persistence and support network that Gaultier possesses, and not all find academic and social homes on campus like she did. However, we heard versions of her story from students across the country and at all types of institutions. The commitment and capacities of students are an essential part of overcoming the barriers to relationship-rich education. This volume is filled with examples of institutional programs and practices that are designed to help students facilitate these connections from their first days in college.

One asset that all institutions possess is the legion of faculty and staff members who are already hard at work mentoring and building conditions to support student peer relationships, despite all of the barriers. Joshua Rodriguez, a thirty-year-old first-generation student at Oakton Community College, had one such experience with an adjunct faculty member who made a profound difference:

> Early in my Calculus 2 class, Professor Arco started getting into really difficult things, and I suddenly began having these feelings like I didn't belong in this class—that my education, what I was trying to achieve, wasn't possible and my goals were just obscenely farther away than I thought they were. I fell a little behind on homework and went to Professor Arco to say that I might have to drop out. He told me, "Joshua, I want you to go home and I don't want you to do the homework tonight. What I want you to do is, I want you to look up imposter syndrome and read about it. Then, right before our next class, come and talk to me." I did that, and I learned that it is extraordinarily common among students. That interaction bolstered my confidence to realize that I'm not alone in this, that everyone has these feelings. And I went from contemplating dropping out and not pursuing my degree to going and getting tutoring help, which is free here at Oakton. I ended up getting an A in the class, and it was entirely because of that one simple interaction. One conversation with Professor Arco was the difference between me not being a student anymore and me being a successful student achieving a 4.0.

That story is not unique. As Randy Bass from Georgetown told us, one of the underappreciated aspects of higher education is "how effing hard most faculty and staff work with students every day. There's so much invisible work going on that is rooted in relationships with students. We need to find ways to tell the full story of faculty and staff work lives. That's an inspiring story of relationships that are pivotal for college students everywhere."

Chapter Three

Making Relationships a Cultural Priority

It is next to impossible to shift the culture overnight. You need to build it from the ground knowing that there's support from the top.

—Mary Deane Sorcinelli, University of Massachusetts Amherst

Across the diverse institutions we visited doing research for this volume, we found powerful evidence of many, many people committed to helping students form relationships that would help make them successful academically and could quite possibly change the trajectory of their careers and lives. We found this to be true at community colleges, research universities, liberal arts colleges, minority-serving institutions, and an online campus, across both the public and private sectors and with admissions standards ranging from open access to the very most selective.

At some institutions, a culture of relationship building seems to be baked into the ethos; a majority of faculty and staff live out a shared mission each day, and the commitment to student success is palpable. But this is not true on most campuses. On some, the research mission dominates everything else. On others, heavy teaching loads and a largely adjunct workforce make it difficult for faculty to connect meaningfully with their students. Cultural divides within colleges and universities are common, too, when, for instance, faculty and student life personnel do not see themselves as partners in the shared work of undergraduate education. Our research leads us to believe that on a majority of campuses, a culture of relationship building is fostered in pockets by certain key individuals, in specific academic departments or disciplines, or in specialized programs such as honors and undergraduate research. The central question, therefore, is, How can institutions be strategic about maximizing opportunities for their students to experience meaningful relationships with faculty, staff, and influential peers? In other words, How can institutions bring the notion of relationship-rich education to scale?

Institutional culture regulates relationship building, for good or ill. Psychologist and university president Thomas Parham of California State University–Dominguez Hills has a profound understanding of the connection between culture and student success. Drawing on the scholarship of Wade Nobles, Parham defines culture as "a complex constellation of mores and values and customs and traditions that provides a general design for living and a pattern for interpreting reality."[1] These values, customs, and traditions are the foundation upon which institutional policies and practices should be based. Parham uses the mantra "transforming lives to transform America," or "T^2" ("transform squared"), to describe the aim of the culture at Dominguez Hills, and he uses the power of stories from students and alumni to illustrate his point.

One story is of an alumna who formerly worked in a travel agency, spending years booking exotic trips for other people. She began to ask clients about their backgrounds and discovered that what all these travelers had in common was a postsecondary degree—an insight that sparked her own quest to enter college. She then approached CSU–Dominguez Hills about admission and was connected to a faculty member who advised her to first begin at a community college. This faculty advisor kept in touch with her throughout her community college studies and continued to advise her following her transfer to Dominguez Hills. The student went on to complete a bachelor's degree and later a graduate degree and now is a cybersecurity technologist for a major national company. She returned to CSU–Dominguez Hills in 2018 to give the first-year convocation address. Hers was a life transformed by a relationship with a caring faculty member and a relationship-rich academic and campus environment. This example illustrates the power of a culture that values students—one at a time, year after year, conversation after conversation—and that leads to enriched lives and stronger communities.

Voices on every campus we visited underscored the importance of institutional culture in fostering relationship building. Vice Provost Randy Bass of Georgetown, who plays a significant role in shaping that institution's culture of teaching and learning, made the point that "relationships are strongest where the structures and the culture are intended to serve the cause of allowing relationships to happen." This idea of *intentionality* in fostering a culture that allows relationships to flourish is key.

When asked why so many first-generation students thrive in the Honors Living-Learning Community at Rutgers University–Newark (described in chapter 5), Assistant Dean for Advisement Engelbert Santana explained: "It's the culture. We need to understand that students are coming here for various reasons, and we need to do as much as we can to ensure this is not a transactional experience. We need to create systems and shift the culture at institutions to build relationships. One of the things I value about Rutgers-Newark is that it is relationship driven."

Indeed, too much about higher education is defined in transactional terms, from the credit hours that lead to degree completion to the amount of effort students need to exert in a class to earn a particular grade. It is thus a radical shift to instead think about higher education from a relational perspective, that is, designing students' pathways through college with the belief that what graduates will value most about college in the end are the significant relationships they formed during those years, rather than whether they earned a B+ or A- in US history.

What elements of an institution's culture allow for a greater chance for students to find meaningful relationships? We believe the following five factors are key.

1. The culture should *value students*. Students should be regarded holistically; they should be encouraged to engage with big questions of meaning and purpose and to find opportunities to build webs of human relationships that allow them to hone their interpersonal skills, be contributing members of groups, and encourage and support others. A culture that values students also sees all students as bringing capacities and assets with them to higher education rather than only deficits and flaws. Above all, an institution should value the students it currently enrolls, not those from some past mythological age when all undergraduates concentrated only on academics, behaved with great decorum, and respected the wisdom of their elders.

2. The culture should *value the efforts faculty and staff put into relationship building*. The institution should hire, retain, promote, and reward people who invest in and value relationships with students. Of course, faculty and staff have multiple allegiances and responsibilities. Faculty have loyalty to their disciplines and are invested in their scholarship; staff manage a multitude of complex offices and programs that must function smoothly. But if an institution is to be intentional about creating a culture that values mentoring and helping students form important connections, it must cultivate a workforce that views one of its principal responsibilities as constructing and maintaining a relationship-rich environment.

3. The culture should *value high-quality teaching*. The classroom remains the most important venue to help students cultivate meaningful relationships that will lead

to academic success. Institutions that are committed to students invest in supporting good teaching, rewarding good teachers, and promoting effective educational practices and relational pedagogies informed by the scholarship of teaching and learning.

4. The culture should *value webs of human interactions.* Students are most likely to develop meaningful relationships in an environment that offers many opportunities for connection. The institution should encourage a climate where everyone on campus, from professors and custodians to deans and office support staff, models mentoring and support for students. To demonstrate their appreciation of the significance of webs of human interactions, institutions need to view developing such a climate as shared work and to recognize that vibrant social networks include many and diverse connections.

5. The culture should *value engagement over prestige.* Much of higher education is prestige oriented, valuing and rewarding, to paraphrase Alexander Astin, *being* smart rather than *becoming* smart.[2] Prestige matters, but relationship-rich experiences are good for all students and are particularly beneficial for students who do not bring with them traditional markers of prestige and privilege, such as top test scores, international travel experience, and access to high-powered career networks. The institution should value metrics of engagement at least as highly as traditional metrics of institutional prestige and should celebrate that meaningful relationships can enable both social mobility and civic leadership.

Following elaboration on the five points above, this chapter will close with a case example of Elon University's work over many decades to nurture a culture focused on student success, engaged learning, and mentoring. This case will illustrate that stewarding campus culture is long-term work, not a quick fix, and involves balancing tensions that naturally exist. Campuses must invest in programs and strategies that are grounded in traditions of welcome and community, permitting relationships to thrive.

A Culture That Values Students

In the wonderful book *Teaching the Whole Student*, David Schoem articulates "an approach and mind-set that looks at students with heart, mind, and spirit, including but also extending beyond their intellectual abilities."[3] Scores of interviewees for our book taught us that truly knowing students means understanding the contexts they come from—their hometowns and neighborhoods, family histories, cultural backgrounds, faith traditions, and more—as well as trying to gain insight into their academic goals and their hopes and fears about college. Coming to understand students is not enough, however; Schoem explains that faculty and staff also need to be open to sharing parts of their own stories: "Relational teaching makes visible the humanity of the teacher and each individual student, as well as the humanity of the class content, subject matter, and text."[4] Making visible the humanity of each student in relation to classmates, teachers, and what is being learned may be the essence of a culture that truly values students.

A culture that values students is oriented toward helping them to encounter the big questions of their lives and taking them beyond seeing education as a series of performances and transactions. Alexander Astin, Helen Astin, and Jennifer Lindholm describe this powerful quest for meaning:

> The "big questions" that preoccupy students are essentially
> spiritual questions: Who am I? What are my most deeply held
> values? Do I have a mission or a purpose in my life? Why am I in

college? What kind of person do I want to become? What sort of world do I want to help create? When we speak of students' "spiritual quests," we are essentially speaking of their efforts to seek answers to such questions.[5]

A culture of valuing students is also inherently connected to cultivating a campus environment in which students will gain practice in navigating their own lives, including forming relationships that will be critical to their success and well-being. In *Practice for Life,* Lee Cuba, Nancy Jennings, Suzanne Lovett, and Joseph Swingle emphasize that

> college is a liminal space and place in which students make lots of decisions that serve as practice for the many more they will make as older adults. This is true of all colleges but especially true of residential colleges, where students live, learn, work, and play in close proximity to one another. College campuses are landscapes on which students are invited to create homes, find advisors and mentors, seek balance, make close friends, and become academically engaged.[6]

College should indeed be practice for life and, like a music practice room, should be a space where students can learn from mistakes, hone their evolving skills, and take purposeful risks to push the boundaries of what they imagine is possible. Creating campus cultures that support and value this critical dimension of the college experience is dependent on faculty and staff who value students as whole human beings.

A Culture That Values the Time Faculty and Staff Put into Relationship Building

John Zubizarreta is one of the nation's leading authorities on honors education and has given a great deal of thought and attention to what constitutes a great undergraduate experience.[7]

During Zubizarreta's long service on the National Collegiate Honors Council, he and his colleagues determined that a core component of honors education is "the mentoring relationship that unfolds in the context of a senior thesis, final project, or capstone." These kinds of interactions do not develop by chance; Zubizarreta insists that institutional culture is essential to effective mentoring:

> An institution needs to commit—I mean whole hog commit—to the importance of mentoring as an institutional cultural priority. If that becomes part of the real, lived mission of the institution, then that institution is going to make mentoring a priority in the type of faculty it goes after—not just hiring willy-nilly because this candidate has ten books and went to an elite university. Our priority is to hire faculty who care and who put teaching at least equal to their other priorities: scholarship and service. But mentoring needs to be a priority institutionally. Otherwise you are going to be struggling to find the kind of faculty who are going to invest in the type of mentoring that we are talking about.

Recruiting, supporting, and rewarding such faculty is important not only for honors education, of course, but for every dimension of the undergraduate experience. When a serious question in the hiring process is whether a prospective faculty member has great potential as a mentor of undergraduates, a culture of mentoring will be advanced.

Hiring the right staff is as important for an institution as hiring the right faculty. Southern New Hampshire University, now enrolling more than ninety thousand online students in more than two hundred degree programs, has come to understand this fact in its burgeoning online program. A typical SNHU student is an adult learner, not a first-time college student, and often works, either full time or part time. President Paul LeBlanc describes SNHU's writing coach and academic advising positions, which augment the faculty role, as their "secret sauce" in the online world:

> *There has to be someone who communicates that you matter. I am drawing on the work of sociologist Gregory Elliott at Brown University. Mattering is the critical piece, especially for first-generation students who have tried college and failed and now they have that baggage to deal with. The person who makes the difference is much more likely to be the advisor or writing coach because they are the ones who can provide that sustained relationship. If I have you in my caseload—if I am your coach—I tend to know what is going on in your world. I have come to know about your family, I have a sense of what your struggles are at school, and I am the one you are most likely to call when you run into a snafu.*

While the vast majority of these coaching and advising sessions at SNHU occur on the telephone, students and their advisors and coaches come to highly value these relationships over time. Academic advisor Margaret O'Leary states, "I think you very quickly learn that what defines culture here is the shared mission to provide affordable, accessible education to students and take away barriers that may have existed for them previously and try to support them being successful."

A Culture That Values High-Quality Teaching

Serge Ballif, an assistant professor of mathematics at Nevada State College, describes the relentless focus on teaching as a defining part of the culture at his institution:

> *It is made very clear in the hiring process that the top priority is teaching. By setting the bar high on teaching, all of the professional development we have goes into teaching. We are always talking students. When someone publishes a research paper we say, "Awesome!" We cheer, and then we move back to students. Our conversations just*

naturally gravitate towards how we can help students. What's working? What's not working? We are always talking students.

Parker Palmer offered the critical insight that even well-intended efforts will not "transform education if we fail to cherish—and challenge—the human heart that is the source of good teaching."[8] Institutions that value students and cultures of relationships must by definition value the hearts, and the classroom practices, of good teachers. Ken Bain's definition of highly effective teachers speaks eloquently to why they are so essential to creating an institutional culture that values relationships with students:

> Highly effective teachers tend to reflect a strong trust in students. They usually believe that students want to learn, and they assume, until proven otherwise, that they can. They often display openness with students and may, from time to time, talk about their own intellectual journey, its ambitions, triumphs, frustrations, and failures, and encourage their students to be similarly reflective and candid. They may discuss how they developed their interests, the major obstacles they have faced in mastering the subject, or some of their secrets for learning particular material. They often discuss openly and enthusiastically their own sense of awe and curiosity about life. Above all, they tend to treat their students with what only can be called simple decency.[9]

Indeed, from the dozens and dozens of faculty members like Professor Ballif we interviewed for this book, the ideas of "teaching from the heart" and "treating students with simple decency" have a powerful ring of truth.

Yet not every institution is (or should be) as single-minded in its dedication to teaching as is Nevada State. Different institutions have different missions. But it is heartbreaking to talk to students who report that throughout the entirety of their undergraduate careers they have not formed a single important relationship with one of their professors. This can be true for many reasons (huge lecture classes and overreliance on part-time faculty are often noted), but one cannot help but have a sense that such a disregard for the quality of the undergraduate experience not only shortchanges students but will also eventually separate institutions from the public trust.

A final dimension to consider when determining whether an institution makes relational teaching a cultural priority is the degree to which it supports faculty tapping into the established and growing body of evidence of what constitutes effective teaching and learning. The American Academy of Arts and Sciences makes this powerful statement:

> The primary determinant of a quality education is the teaching and learning relationship between faculty and students. Effective student/faculty interactions are correlated with increased retention and completion rates, better grades and standardized test scores, and higher career and graduate school aspirations. Quite simply, students learn more and fail less when faculty members consult and utilize a large and growing body of research about effective teaching methods and make connections with students. Yet, despite the high stakes now associated with undergraduate education, most institutions pay too little attention to these findings.[10]

If the commitment of institutions to high-quality teaching and learning is to be more than lip service, investments must be made in worthwhile faculty development programs to help faculty grow in their teaching and mentoring roles. (The Teaching and Learning Institute's Students as Learners and Teachers program of Bryn Mawr College and Haverford College profiled in chapter 5 is a remarkable example.) And despite some efforts to prepare graduate students for the professoriate,[11] such as Preparing Future Faculty of the Council of Graduate Schools, the majority of faculty members still begin their first teaching positions with insufficient pedagogical preparation. This is one of the great structural deficiencies of American higher education, and it is exacerbated because many institutions do not invest in serious mentoring programs for new faculty; furthermore, contingent faculty are often left entirely to their own devices.

A Culture That Values Webs of Human Interaction

In their book *Everybody Matters,* Bob Chapman and Raj Sisodia posit that the vast majority of employees in the United States "go home every day feeling that they work for an organization that doesn't listen to or care about them.... but instead sees them merely as functions or objects, as a means to the success of the organization."[12] In contrast with that alienating experience, Chapman and Sisodia call for a very different institutional ethos that values all employees: "In the end, it is about truly caring for every precious human being whose lives we touch. It is about including everybody, not just the fortunate few or the exceptionally talented."[13]

That is as true in colleges and universities as it is in the corporate world. If our institutions do not honor the contributions of all faculty and staff, our students lose out on powerful relationships: "Every person on a college campus has the potential to be a teacher and a mentor, and all should be supported by strong institutional expectations and commitments."[14] In order to create a culture that values caring, inclusion, and relationships, *all* employees must understand and believe in the higher purposes of their work—must believe that they shape a learning environment that can and will be transformational in the lives of students. People who clean classrooms and residence halls, cafeteria staff, office personnel, and the myriad employees who supervise student workers often turn out to be important mentors, teachers, and guides.

Oftentimes, simple actions can demonstrate caring and inclusion in the cause of relationship building. Two examples from the innovative Honors Living-Learning Community (HLLC) at Rutgers University–Newark illustrate how seemingly routine interactions can be made significant. Assistant Dean Engelbert Santana describes how the admissions process for the HLLC includes everyone in this academic community:

> We invite everyone on campus to participate in the large group interview process, from the chancellor's office team to faculty, staff, groundskeepers, police officers, community members, and alumni. For a lot of our students this interview meeting is their first interaction with Rutgers-Newark. They are going through an interview process for a competitive program, but it doesn't feel like that. It feels like a welcoming community. So whether a student is admitted to the HLLC or not, they may later come across a faculty or staff member who may say, "I remember you from the large group interview. I'm glad you're here at the university."

What could feel like an intimidating admissions interview instead initiates a process of welcome and belonging for students and empowers faculty and staff to begin building relationships before undergraduates even enroll at the university.

This approach to admissions reflects the philosophy of the inaugural dean of the HLLC, Timothy K. Eatman, who speaks from a core belief: "Any student who is able to develop healthy and inspiring relationships with faculty or other folks on campus will thrive." Eatman understands the power of simple moments to help students develop a sense of agency and belonging. He describes walking across campus and encountering an HLLC student who was standing with a friend: "The friend was looking down or away like she has no access to me, so I asked my student, 'Who is your friend?' And he replied, 'This is Regina.' And then I said, 'Hi, Regina. How are you? Are you a student at Rutgers

University–Newark?' Regina replied, 'Yes, I am,' to which I responded, 'Well, I am a professor here. So you are my student.'"

Powerful moments like this build institutional culture to support students' sense of belonging and search for relationships. Colleges and universities require moments like these to occur daily to create the cultures that campuses need.

Faculty and staff who touch student lives require training and investment to ensure they can provide support as effectively as possible. When Eric Hofmann, assistant dean of academic affairs and director of the Center for Teaching and Learning at LaGuardia Community College, describes the ethos of the campus, he includes the professional development of frontline staff in his definition: "This is a learning college. It's a learning institution. We're also reaching out to frontline staff across the college, including in our adult and continuing education program, asking how we can help build your communication skills, help you interact with students, and understand your emotional intelligence. It's developing them because they also touch our students. And it's important to create an entire environment that supports students."

With a staff-to-faculty ratio of two to one on many campuses, institutions must invest not just in the faculty but also in the larger pool of potential mentors who are on the front lines of creating a sense of belonging and welcome for students.

Recognizing that support staff do not always get the attention they deserve for mentoring and supporting students, Georgetown graduate Febin Bellamy created Unsung Heroes in 2016. Bellamy did not take the typical path to Georgetown, having graduated high school with a 1.2 grade point average. Bellamy's desire to become serious about his future and to change his work ethic followed his father's stroke soon after Bellamy completed high school. He enrolled in Rockland Community College and simultaneously worked at Wendy's, performing tasks like cleaning floors—the beginning of a process of discovery that "every single job has dignity."

Following a successful experience at Rockland Community College, Bellamy transferred to Georgetown. He had dreamed of studying there, but the reality of life on campus as a low-income, African American transfer student did not match his hopes: "I felt invisible and alone." Then, late one night, he met Oneill Batchelor, a longtime Georgetown employee who cleaned the business school building where Bellamy frequently studied. "Meeting Oneill changed everything about my experience at Georgetown," says Bellamy. They developed a bond rooted in their shared experience as immigrants and their common interests in food, religion, and sports.

As their relationship developed, Bellamy learned that Batchelor also often felt invisible at Georgetown, like workers on many campuses who keep the campus clean, safe, and running smoothly. To honor the contributions of his "brother" at Georgetown, after graduation Bellamy created Unsung Heroes, a media company that helps college and university students share the stories of people like Batchelor who have had profound but often unrecognized influences on their experiences as undergraduates. Unsung Heroes also raises funds to support entrepreneurial activities by the people profiled, including seed capital that enabled Batchelor to establish his own catering business.[15]

A Culture That Values Engagement over Prestige

President Parham of CSU–Dominguez Hills made another fundamental point about institutional culture in speaking about "shifting the institutional dialogue in higher education from how elite you can become to how engaged you can become." The measures of prestige are well known to everyone in higher education circles and to much of the public: endowment size, funded research, student selectivity as measured by grade point average and standardized tests, alumni giving, numbers of faculty with MacArthur Genius Grants, and so on.

Parham calls for leadership to distinguish between "pride factors" (which get students interested in and admitted to institutions) and "human factors" (which help students to connect and succeed at institutions). Colleges and university officials are skilled at playing the prestige game, and various rankings and ratings have all too often become the tail wagging the dog, influencing strategic planning and priority setting, fundraising, and the agendas of trustees, senior leaders, and faculty. What a fundamental transformation might take place in higher education if everyone engaged in the endeavor placed a premium on how well our institutions engage students! Indeed, a recent report from the Stanford Graduate School of Education, "A 'Fit' over Rankings," states boldly that "engagement in college is more important than where you attend."[16] Lynn Swaner astutely identifies the challenge: intentionality. "Most colleges and universities have engagement as a priority in their institutional mission statements, but it requires intentionality, diplomacy, and (for lack of a better term) grit to translate engagement into the dominant models of teaching and learning at colleges and universities."[17]

So what could institutional intentionality and grit look like? Some possibilities:

- Regularly reviewing the data institutions collect about student engagement and relationship-rich high-impact educational practices, including the results of tools like the National Survey of Student Engagement; observing trends over time; and setting specific institutional goals to address inequities and perceived undesirable trends
- Ensuring full-time faculty teach first-year core classes and providing support for those teachers so classes are engaging, creative, challenging, and relational

- Developing cocurricular transcripts to both document and value student participation in meaningful and interactive experiences outside of the classroom
- Developing systems to track student advising and mentoring engagements, to identify good practices and gaps in involvement, and to support and reward the people who do this essential work
- Monitoring investments in faculty development to support the adoption of engaged and relational pedagogies and curricula
- Utilizing e-portfolios to assist students in reflecting on and integrating their most critical engagements and relationships in their undergraduate experiences

These practices, of course, involve hard and deliberate work. But unless the necessity of developing and monitoring practices like these are included in the agendas of faculty meetings and governing boards, cultures of relationship and engagement will not be sustained.

Case Example: Elon University

Thanks in part to George Keller's book *Transforming a College*,[18] the narrative of Elon University's transformation from a small regional college to a midsize national university has been well documented, and Elon's strategies and decisions have been studied extensively. A key element of that story is thoughtful planning and financing based on a clearly defined institutional mission and a culture committed to student success through engagement and relationships.

Delegations of faculty, administrators, and trustees from all over the world have visited Elon over the past two decades to assess for themselves how the experience of Elon's transformation might apply to their own campuses. Much of what they take away from their study of Elon is the importance of the institution's culture to its transformation. Four lessons emerge as the most significant.

Culture Is about the Long Haul, Not the Quick Fix

Elon traces its culture of engaged learning and student success to the 1970s, decades before the phrase *engaged learning* became part of the common parlance of higher education. When policies of required chapel attendance were falling away nationally, including at Elon, President J. Fred Young and his faculty colleagues began to search for contemporary approaches to animate the institution's mission and values, giving rise to new, experiential, relationship-rich learning opportunities on campus and what eventually became known as the Elon Experiences (community service, global study, leadership, internships, and undergraduate research). An experiential learning requirement was established in 1984, and in the following decade Elon faculty radically restructured the curriculum by awarding four credit hours for most classes in order to permit faculty time to teach fewer courses and add depth and interactive learning experiences to each course, both keys to the culture of relationship building across campus. When asked how the university became a leader in engaged, experiential learning, Provost Steven House notes, "We've been creating our culture for a very long time, with each new piece building on the established foundation."

Because a culture of engaged learning has been part of the institution's ethos for nearly five decades and coincided with a period of dramatic growth in the size of the student body, Elon was also able to recruit hundreds of new faculty, staff, administrators, and students who were attracted by Elon's learning-centered mission and culture of engagement and relationship building, which became powerfully self-reinforcing. And yet the new faculty and staff brought fresh perspectives to the mix. President Connie Ledoux Book notes, for example, that when Elon recently made a $150 million investment in new residential facilities, designing those facilities to incorporate faculty-in-residence apartments was greatly informed by faculty and staff members' own undergraduate experiences on residential campuses.

Stewardship of Culture Involves Balancing Healthy Tensions

Most institutional cultures, including Elon's, are neither monolithic nor static; indeed, they are complex and dynamic. While continuing to advance a culture of engaged learning and student success, Elon simultaneously raised academic standards across the board, benchmarking the institution to other campuses with chapters of Phi Beta Kappa and top accreditations for professional schools. And at the same time the institution made significant investments to support the scholarly work of its young faculty (as most of its new tenure-track faculty hired in response to growth were at the assistant professor level). The challenge became one of balancing new emphases on higher academic standards and faculty scholarship with a long-standing culture of student engagement and relational teaching.

Key to keeping this institutional change in balance was a two-year conversation among the faculty which resulted in the adoption of "The Elon Teacher-Scholar Statement."[19] As discussions unfolded, faculty had critical conversations about balancing emerging tensions within the institutional culture. Faculty determined that Elon should maintain a primary commitment to excellence in undergraduate teaching and mentoring while advancing faculty scholarship through new investments recommended by a presidential task force on scholarship. And while faculty were excited to advance the more rigorous academic standards that professional accrediting bodies and Phi Beta Kappa expected, they wanted to meet these standards while maintaining their long-term commitment to engaged, experiential education and high-quality teaching. In other words, the Elon community sought ways to weave new institutional aspirations into a long-standing and valued culture of relationship-rich student learning.

Such high-level, deliberate, and intentional conversations are essential to the maintenance of a strong institutional culture. Provost Steven House is fond of quoting a line from the presidential task force on scholarship: "In truth, there is no 'old' or 'new' Elon. Every year brings a new set of challenges, and the university—like its fabled namesake the Phoenix—builds itself anew in response to those challenges."[20] Maintaining a strong institutional culture requires careful reflection, attention, and action by all members of the campus community.

Nourishing Culture Requires Consistent Financial Investments

Elon is a tuition-dependent institution with a comparably modest endowment that until recently dedicated much of its fundraising efforts to expanding the physical campus and developing new academic programs. (Building endowment for student financial aid has become the principal fundraising priority in the last decade.) The culture-reinforcing initiatives noted above (investing in high-impact practices and academic quality, expanding the residential campus, reducing the student-faculty ratio significantly, and more) have required hundreds of millions of dollars in investments. How has Elon accomplished this without a multi-billion-dollar endowment? The answer is simple to recite but hard to accomplish: principally by, first, selecting its priorities judiciously and ensuring they are in line with the institutional mission and culture and, second, investing discretionary resources (both institutional and dollars raised) in those key priorities year after year. In other words, to see what an institution truly values, follow the money.

Provost House tells of a visitor to Elon whose president had given him $50,000 and instructions to "create an undergraduate research program like Elon's" (including participation of 27 percent of the undergraduate student body, support for faculty mentors, and funding for student participation in national conferences), only to be advised by the director of Elon's undergraduate research program that he would need another $1.5 million—and twenty years. Without unexpected windfalls, most tuition-dependent institutions do not have vast sums to invest in new programs in one fell swoop. Elon's story illustrates that focused investments over time can leverage high quality, relationship-focused, high-impact practices. But they cannot be created by edict or overnight.

Traditions of Welcome and Community Matter

President Book notes that "what initially stages a culture that values relationships is the welcome you provide." Many institutions have tone-setting traditions that communicate the message "We care about each other at this place." Book sees Elon's move-in weekend for first-year students and New Student Convocation as key for communicating important messages to students and their families. A smooth move-in process and carefully designed orientation program communicate that the university has thought through potential challenges to belonging and wants to remove barriers to feeling welcomed. A formal outdoor convocation ceremony with faculty in academic regalia signals that something new and important is about to begin; emphasizes the academic values that undergird life at the institution; and powerfully communicates, both visually and orally, that the faculty will be in partnership with students on their educational journeys. And because every person on the campus—from carpenters and faculty to electricians and deans—participates in the welcome process, a palpable sense of the community coming together to support students is created. In times of institutional tension and even conflict, these moments of common purpose and community are the ties that bind.

The ultimate test of institutional leadership—whether by faculty, staff, trustees, or administrators—is the stewardship of institutional culture. Institutional cultures are both precious and fragile. It takes years to build a strong, positive culture, but culture can be seriously damaged in the span of a few months by a sudden veering of direction in pursuit of ill-considered priorities or a lack of attention to the small details of institutional life that signal that people care and are paying attention. To build the culture of a relationship-rich campus requires the buy-in of hundreds, if not thousands, of caring, committed people; constant reinforcement of the message that relationships matter; and reward and recognition of the efforts of faculty and staff who do the everyday work of connecting with students.

Chapter Four

Creating Relationship-Rich Classrooms

What I have tried to do in my classrooms is communicate to students that I am available to them, but also to create the conditions in the classroom so that students will talk with one another. As teachers, we are being measured and evaluated all the time on things that don't have to do with what I think are central human values, like our ability to be full human beings in relation to one another.

—David M. Levy, University of Washington

The classroom, whether physical or virtual, is the primary point of contact between institutions and undergraduates, so it is the single most important site for students to experience welcome and care, to be inspired to learn, to build webs of relationships, and to ask questions of meaning and purpose. This chapter begins by focusing on the nature of those faculty-student relationships and then goes on to consider how faculty can leverage their role in the classroom by cultivating student-student interactions that foster educationally meaningful relationships. Classroom communities can be contentious and difficult, so we address some of the challenges of teaching and learning in divisive times. We conclude by exploring ways faculty can work together to create curricula and environments that sustain educational relationships beyond the individual classroom. First, though, two stories from our research:

Mays Imad, a professor of biology at Pima Community College, had an epiphany one ordinary day in class:

> I was lecturing when I realized that I was staring at my students and they were staring into space. That took me back to my time as a student in 2003 when I was trying to learn molecular biology while also worrying if my family in Iraq was still alive. It dawned on me that I could continue to lecture and get through the material and check off all the learning objectives, or I could really attend to the students who were in class with me. So I started to ask my students, "What is it that you want?" I learned that they wanted the science, but they didn't want it in a vacuum. They wanted science in relation to the world and to their lives. They wanted to connect with science—and with me.

Imad began to imagine her classroom as a learning sanctuary; she transformed her classroom through what she calls "relational teaching."[1] She aims to build trust and connections with her students through personal stories and interactions in and out of class, but, even more significant, she strives to build relationships among her students because she knows that she does not have the time necessary to work one-on-one with all of her students. She uses class time to introduce students to "peer-to-peer mentoring because once they get the taste of it, they want more—and they organize their own study groups and support each other outside of class."

Echoing Imad, Bryan Dewsbury, an assistant professor of biology at the University of Rhode Island, asserts that relationships are at the very center of every higher education classroom. Although Dewsbury often teaches 150 students in each section of introduction to biology, every activity in his classroom is designed to build "a community of scholars" among his students and between him and his students. Dewsbury begins to create this relationship-rich classroom culture before the course even starts, not only by poring over institutional data about his students so he can better understand their educational and social backgrounds but also by assigning his students to write brief essays to introduce themselves to him in the style of a "This I Believe"[2] statement that articulates their purposes for studying biology. These stories help Dewsbury come to know his students both as a group and as individuals and then to craft his pedagogy around their particular goals and needs: "If I notice a lot of low confidence among students one semester, I can do things that research shows will inspire confidence and will build a sense of belonging." Throughout the semester, Dewsbury challenges and encourages his students during class time and in one-on-one exchanges out of the classroom to continue to reflect on their purposes for studying biology and to connect with their peers in ways that support their learning.

Both Dewsbury and Imad illustrate the centrality of faculty in relationship-rich classrooms. Not all classroom relationships can or should run through a faculty member, but the faculty member's course design, formal pedagogy, and informal interactions with students will shape the quality and quantity of both student-faculty and student-student relationships in the classroom. Students at residential colleges and universities may have opportunities outside of the curriculum to develop relationships with faculty and peers, but even in these settings the classroom is the central place for interactions focused on learning. And most students in higher education today are *not* living on campus. As Danette Barber of Nevada State College explains, "Because right now we're a 100 percent commuter campus, making connections can sometimes be very difficult for students. Most of our students have off-campus jobs, and a lot of them have familial obligations to take care of children or siblings or parents. Class time is *the* prime opportunity for building educational relationships." Karen Stout, president of Achieving the Dream, a nonprofit organization that helps community college students succeed, reinforces this reality at community colleges: "Our faculty have always been and will always be the first and most frequent point of ongoing contact with our students."[3] Even in a profoundly student-centered residential campus, faculty are the fulcrum that enables or constrains educational relationships.

Student-Faculty Relationships

For more than fifty years, scholars have documented the importance of student-faculty interactions to enhance learning, completion, motivation, critical thinking, career aspirations, belonging, and self-confidence. A synthesis of the literature concluded: "For most students most of the time, the more interaction with faculty the better."[4] Indeed, student-faculty interactions are the single most significant factor in positive educational outcomes for students of color and are also especially significant for first-generation students.[5] Recent research also demonstrates that classroom interactions with faculty and student peers contribute positively to student well-being and that faculty need not "go beyond their professional role" to support student well-being— they need only "give more attention to the social dimensions of learning that are within their role."[6]

Many higher education labor practices do *not* reflect the centrality of faculty in achieving student learning goals and the broader aims of the academy. Research indicates that faculty in full-time positions are more likely than part-time faculty to use active learning pedagogies that support student-student classroom interactions, and that tenure-track faculty are more likely than adjunct faculty to have regular and meaningful interactions with their students.[7] Community college students also may have lower long-term academic outcomes when they are taught by part-time faculty.[8] Yet in 2016, some 47 percent of US faculty held part-time appointments.[9] No matter how dedicated and skillful part-time faculty are, "their working conditions make it nearly impossible for them to be as involved as their full-time peers in the lives of students and to provide these students with similar support outside of class."[10]

Cultural, racial, gender, and other differences within the classroom can also complicate teaching, learning, and relationship building. Undergraduate student demographics are changing rapidly, even as faculty and staff composition remains relatively stable.[11] The educational benefits of diverse college classrooms and cross-racial interactions among undergraduates are well documented,[12] but those benefits do not make engaging across differences easy for either students or faculty. Knowing and caring about diversity are not enough. Faculty need to take responsibility for creating classroom environments that encourage meaningful interactions with and among students.[13] Laura Rendón's concept of *validation* provides a strong foundation for approaching this challenging work.[14] Faculty (and other "institutional agents") initiate validation by interacting with students in ways that convey belief in their ability to succeed in and beyond college; this often involves setting high expectations and establishing a caring, supportive environment that enables students to learn, make mistakes, and pick themselves back up to try again. Validation helps students "acquire a confident, motivating, 'I can do it' attitude, believe in their inherent capacity to learn, become excited about learning, feel a part of the learning community, and feel cared about as a person, not just a student."[15]

Even when validation allows strong student-faculty relationships to blossom, there is no simple recipe for successful student-faculty classroom interactions. Instead, a wide range of creative approaches have been developed and adapted by faculty to cultivate educationally purposeful relationships with students in all kinds of situations, from small seminars to fully online courses and even large lectures. This array of practices suggests that building personal connections and communicating both challenge and support are essential to productive student-faculty relationships.

Building Personal Connections

At nearly every institution, careful attention is paid to the first-year experience in college because research so clearly demonstrates that how students start matters.[16] Yet for most students, even for those who remain at the same institution for four years, the experience of being in college is punctuated by a series of new beginnings, including the launch of each new term: "Students don't just start college and then finish it. They start and then re-start college many times."[17] The beginning of each course marks a new opportunity for students to develop the kinds of purposeful relationships with faculty that will enhance motivation, learning, and belonging.

Faculty at Oakton Community College have drawn on a range of research-informed practices to create the Faculty Project for Student Persistence, an initiative aimed to cultivate a relationship-rich classroom and thereby to support both more learning in a particular course and more students continuing their studies at Oakton semester to semester. Faculty in the Persistence Project, as it is colloquially known, commit to integrate four steps into their pedagogical plans for the first three weeks of the semester:

1. Learn their students' names
2. Return an assignment to each student with formative, success-orientated feedback early in the term
3. Articulate high academic standards for the course but also send a clear message that students who struggle are not doomed, because opportunities exist for academic support outside of class

4. Meet one-on-one with each student for a ten- to fifteen-minute conversation

Individual faculty and departments adapt these four steps to fit their own disciplinary and teaching contexts. Data from the Persistence Project illustrate the power of this systematic approach to starting courses well: students in Persistence Project course sections are more than 24 percent more likely than their peers to return to Oakton the next semester, and the positive effect is even greater for students who identify as African American.[18]

Step 4, one-on-one meetings, is perhaps the most unusual and daunting aspect of the Persistence Project. Oakton students, particularly those who are new to higher education, report being "intimidated" and "kind of scared" by the requirement to meet individually with faculty members. However, Allison Wallin, who is studying environmental science, explained that "having to have that meeting creates a relationship that you can build on later in the semester if you ever need to talk to them about a problem. And it makes it easier to speak up in class as well." Gina Roxas, a student planning to transfer to earn her bachelor's degree in environmental biology, describes one such meeting with a biology professor as "very key to my education here because she not only showed that she cared about her students but also was well versed in the resources available to support students, which helped me connect with the honors program and a science mentor and also scholarship opportunities."

Oakton faculty also find the one-on-one meetings challenging because they take so much time during the busy start to a semester. Yet, like their students, they see this as time well spent. Camille Harrison, a professor of Arabic and French, believes that her individual meetings enhance student motivation in her classes because students know she cares about their learning and also because she can use information gleaned from these conversations to emphasize topics and themes that particularly interest her students. Holly Graff, a professor of philosophy and chair of the humanities department, expresses surprise at how much difference these meetings have made in her colleagues' classrooms and her own:

> *I've been teaching here a long time, and I still am in contact with some of my students from twenty years ago, but when I added the one-on-one conferences, it transformed me and my teaching. My departmental colleagues have said the same thing. I am not just getting to know the students with whom I might have the greatest affinities; instead, I am getting to know all my students, and there's a big difference between those two things.*

One-on-one meetings are not feasible for all faculty or courses. At Oakton many faculty teach five or more sections each semester, making it hard to meet all students individually near the start of the term. The intention of the Persistence Project, however, is not to create a one-size-fits-all approach but rather to cultivate a classroom and campus culture that encourages and values student-faculty interactions. Every student who has even one of these meetings learns that faculty at Oakton are available to support and challenge, helping to counter the imposter syndrome that pervades so many college campuses. And when students talk with each other, those who have benefited from the Persistence Project encourage their peers to approach faculty to ask questions and to get help. Even students who have not had meaningful interactions with faculty know that such relationships are possible.

The Persistence Project also echoes the research demonstrating that the quality, more than the quantity, of student-faculty interaction is key.[19] Small steps can yield large results. For instance, the systematic use of name tents in high-enrollment biology courses has been shown by scholars at Arizona State University to have statistically significant positive results on student motivation and learning and also makes it more likely that students will seek help from their faculty. Faculty do not need to memorize student names to achieve these outcomes; the practice of having students make and use simple name tents and then faculty intentionally calling students by name, when possible, seems to be sufficient. Students in this study report: "When I feel that personal connection with the instructor, it makes me want to do better in the class as well. It's almost as if I'm extra accountable" and "I feel like I'm just a face in the crowd most of the time, even in classes where the teacher is really excited about teaching and helping students understand. Knowing names makes me feel more noticed and welcome."[20]

Communicating in Ways That Challenge and Support

Manda Williamson teaches an online introduction to psychology course at the University of Nebraska with an enrollment of seven hundred students. She not only instructs her students in the foundations of her discipline but also explicitly communicates with them about how psychological research—particularly efficacy interventions that aim to help students develop the ability to produce desired results in specific contexts[21]—guides her teaching and assessment strategies. She begins class by sending students a letter explaining a bit about her background, articulating her expectations of them, and affirming that she is confident they will succeed in the course if they work purposefully and persist through struggle. She threads that same message of challenge and belonging through every message she sends her students. This efficacy-centered approach to online teaching consistently produces twice the rate of student success as in prior online versions of the course or in comparable face-to-face courses at the university. Williamson's communications are carefully crafted to help her seven hundred students believe that she supports them and that they are capable of doing what it takes to achieve their academic goals in her class and at Nebraska. Every week, she emphasizes that students have the ability to succeed: "College will not get the best of you if you have the courage to ask those you trust for assistance."

Serge Ballif also stresses student self-efficacy in his calculus courses at Nevada State College by using "specifications grading"[22] to establish transparent, high standards for student performance coupled with the promise that all students can learn if they are willing to work hard. Students take frequent quizzes, which they can retake in Ballif's office if they do not pass. This means that struggling students will interact with him, allowing him to give personalized feedback and encouragement to the students who need it most:

> I've had multiple instances where I've managed to get students to actually thrive in calculus when at first they were having trouble even staying afloat. One student failed to pass each of the first fifteen quizzes of the semester, but she would come to see me every single time and we would go over practice problems. I must admit I didn't have terribly high hopes for her because she had some really significant gaps in her knowledge, but she was putting in the time and she kept coming to see me. Then in the last third of the semester she managed to pass most of the quizzes on the first try, so she went from a student who I would have seen as borderline or failing to one who learned a lot of calculus and ended up succeeding in the course.

Such a time-intensive approach to grading may not be sustainable for all faculty or courses, but it underscores the power of regular, purposeful, and affirming student-faculty interactions to convey expectations and belonging in the classroom—and to encourage deep learning by all students.

Similar results have been found from a light-touch intervention in large economics courses at public universities in California. This approach draws on research in behavioral economics, education, and social psychology to significantly affect student learning and persistence while minimizing the amount of time a faculty member must invest: "By conveying beliefs in students' abilities to succeed in the course and in college more generally, college instructors have an important way to directly and indirectly contribute to college success: directly through the intended transfer of content knowledge and/or skills and indirectly through boosting students' sense of self-efficacy."[23]

In the light-touch study, a faculty member sent each student in a high-enrollment introductory economics course two personalized emails during the semester with the purpose of providing tailored information about (1) the student's performance in the course to date, (2) strategies and approaches that help students learn in the class, and (3) the availability of the professor and other resources to support the student's success in the course. Students who received these emails scored higher on exams, homework, and final course grades than students in the control group who did not. Some students who received these emails even responded to express gratitude to the professor for caring enough to email or to say that they would try to work harder for the remainder of the semester.[24]

Taylor Schlesinger, a math student and academic peer tutor at LaGuardia Community College, emphasizes the importance of such messages for students. Early in her time at LaGuardia, she had an English professor who started class one day by commenting on something he said happened too often:

"Near the end of the semester, one of my best students is going to stop coming to class because they feel overwhelmed with all the pressure and they are really scared that they are going to do poorly." And he went on

to say, "I want to assure that student to keep coming to class, even if you missed an assignment or feel like you didn't do well on an essay, because it's going to be okay. Come see me, don't just disappear."

That simple but powerful message is so important for students to hear, Schlesinger believes, because it reminds them that their professors are allies in, not obstacles to, their learning and success in college. Indeed, Manda Williamson at Nebraska conveys just such messages to her online students every term, and, as with Schlesinger and her peers, their academic performance demonstrates the effectiveness of student-faculty relationships in supporting and challenging students to succeed.

Student-Student Classroom Interactions

The foundational book *How College Affects Students* concludes that student-student interactions are "positively related to general learning, cognition, racial identity, intellectual/academic self-concept, autonomy, well-being, moral development, retention/graduation, and expected career outcomes."[25] In a range of STEM courses, active learning and peer-based pedagogies have been demonstrated to produce deeper learning as well as enhanced performance, motivation, and belonging.[26] David Scobey, director of the independent project Bringing Theory to Practice, synthesizes this research and his own experiences with adult learners to conclude, "These horizontal peer-to-peer relationships are the ones that keep students—especially students who are marginalized—from letting each other fail."

However, simply having students talk with peers or be active in the classroom is not enough. As with student-faculty interactions, the quality and purpose of student-student work is more important than the quantity. Faculty need to both design and communicate about constructive and meaningful peer interactions. For instance, Siskanna Naynaha, professor of English and coordinator for writing across the curriculum at CSU–Dominguez Hills, has a section of every syllabus "that explains not only that we're going to be doing group work pretty much every single day but also why we are doing it—the importance of it to students' success—and laying some of the groundwork for how I expect students to conduct themselves in those groups." In general, peer-to-peer classroom learning is most effective when it is guided by two principles: (1) positive interdependence, meaning that the work is demanding enough that collective effort is essential for students to succeed, and (2) individual accountability, meaning that student learning will be evaluated at least in part independently.[27]

University of Rhode Island biology professor Bryan Dewsbury conceives of student-student classroom interactions in another elemental way: that classroom experiences with peers will translate into the relationships that will help students study together productively *outside* of class. For instance, after asking students to predict their scores on their first examination and then anonymously plotting students' expected scores against their (typically lower) earned scores, he asks students, "What does it really mean to understand something?" He then has students imagine themselves walking down the street when a late-night TV comedian pops up to say to them, "I really want to understand how proteins fold." Dewsbury probes: "Can you talk them through that process, out of the blue, without your textbook or without Google? Can you do that from start to finish?" He encourages students to play that late-night comedian for each other as they study, asking for clear and notes-free explanations of key course material.

Dewsbury explains that such peer-to-peer conversations are critical because "students have come out of a system where knowing meant repeating something an authority told them. Especially at the first-year level, there's a lot of bad high school habits being repeated: read the whole chapter the night before, highlight everything that's in bold, memorize, memorize, memorize, and then close the book and go to sleep." Dewsbury's goal is to have students abandon that old model in favor of leveraging the power of learning with peers.

Even with a creative and charismatic professor like Dewsbury, however, students do not always eagerly take to active learning and peer-based pedagogies. Indeed, Tekla Nicholas, a researcher who studies student success, recalls that a decade ago many Florida International University students complained about active learning: "I wish my teacher would just teach. Now I'm expected to learn everything on my own." This kind of student resistance and "social loafing" is often attributed to deficits in students' attitudes, motivation, or study skills.[28] However, a comprehensive study of peer learning in college STEM classrooms concludes: "Our data raise the possibility that perhaps instead of students being lazy or unmotivated, students face barriers such as anxiety about group work, low perceived value of peer discussion for their learning, or contending with other students in the group who are dominating."[29]

These findings put the onus on faculty to structure meaningful student-student interactions that stipulate well-defined, rotating roles so that all students are required to take (and relinquish) the initiative, that schedule time to develop group cohesion, and that assign complex and open-ended challenges that will require collaboration to address successfully. Well-trained learning assistants and other student leaders in a course can help make peer pedagogies even more effective (more on learning assistants in chapter 5). Indeed, a study comparing face-to-face, fully online, and hybrid (50 percent face-to-face, 50 percent online) large introductory biology courses at Florida International University found traditional face-to-face lecture sections had the lowest student performance of the three formats. This study concludes: "Active-learning exercises done in teams and with support from undergraduate learning assistants and the instructor" proved to be the most important factor for positive student outcomes, particularly for students of color, regardless of whether the course was online, hybrid, or face-to-face.[30] And the more students experience well-designed collaborative pedagogies, the more readily they will engage in them. Tekla Nicholas explains that, at FIU,

> Over time, we have seen students shift their responses to active learning and structured peer work. Now students are saying, "This really helps me to learn. I am working harder. I am learning more. And I'm being more successful." Explaining to them what this process was all about and their hearing that same message about active learning in chemistry class and in English class and in biology class was a part of a huge cultural shift.

Purposeful peer classroom interactions not only enhance learning and belonging, but they also contribute to student confidence and self-efficacy. Samantha Paskvan, a biochemistry student at the University of Washington, illustrates the trajectory of a student who feels empowered by positive peer and faculty relationships:

> The teachers in our biology department are really interested in active learning, and I found that that type of learning really resonated with me. It's very collaborative working in small groups and having lots of discussion during lecture. I had one professor in genetics the fall quarter of my junior year who dedicated so much time to his students and was really clear about expectations and just was the most phenomenal teacher I ever had. At the very end of the quarter, I just walked up to him after the last lecture and I said, "Thank you so much for a great quarter. Are you accepting undergraduate research students?"

Samantha Paskvan's reflection echoes a mushrooming body of research about the centrality of social and relational learning for undergraduate education. The eleven High-Impact Practices first identified by George Kuh and then popularized by the Association of American Colleges and Universities all require that students work closely with peers and faculty (and often others) as they learn.[31] A large multi-institutional study of college writing similarly concluded that students find assignments to be most "meaningful" when they experience "writing as a social act" that, while usually completed individually, involves deep connection with peers, instructors, and an authentic audience.[32] As the scholar bell hooks has observed: "Learning and talking together, we break the notion that our experience of gaining knowledge is private, individualistic, and competitive. By choosing and fostering dialogue, we engage mutually in a learning partnership."[33]

Conflicts in Classroom Relationships

The Students as Learners and Teachers (SaLT) program (profiled in chapter 5) of Bryn Mawr College and Haverford College pairs carefully selected and prepared students to partner as consultants to Bryn Mawr and Haverford faculty about their teaching, including spending significant time in the classroom observing professors in action as well as debriefing about what they saw and suggesting strategies for improvement. Aside from the enormous personal and professional growth both faculty and students derive from the program, another overarching benefit is apparent: the seeding of a healthy culture at Bryn Mawr and Haverford to talk about complex classroom dynamics. Former Haverford president Kim Benston noted that the major issues in our changing world, especially political and societal divisiveness and racism, have brought new challenges and tensions to the nation's classrooms. And yet the depth of the conversations between SaLT consultants and their faculty partners is helping faculty negotiate this complexity with greater confidence: "We have this history of an ongoing modality of faculty and student engagement. It gives us a head start on a really complex moment in educational history. We don't back down or minimize the challenges. They are real. SaLT is not a magic pill, but it's a significant head start."

Courses and classrooms offer rich environments for meaningful relationships, but they also can be places of conflict, resistance, and exclusion. Many of these conflicts flare from long-term challenges that students face in classrooms. The 2015 Amherst Uprising was sparked by outside events but quickly came to focus on what one alum described as the all-too-common experience of students of color: "I did not reach my full potential because I felt ignored, misunderstood and therefore could not get the support I needed."[34] And the very same thing can be said by lesbian, gay, bisexual, transgender, queer or questioning, intersex, and asexual or allied (LGBTQIA) students and other individuals and groups who experience marginalization or alienation on campus.[35] These deep challenges are vexing, but across the country faculty and institutions are partnering with students to develop comprehensive ways to ameliorate long-term inequities. At Amherst College, the Being Human in STEM course and program (which now has spread to other campuses) "aims to foster a more inclusive, supportive STEM community by helping students, faculty, and staff collaboratively develop a framework to understand and navigate diverse identities in the classroom, lab, and beyond."[36]

This combination of strong student-faculty and student-student relationships, clear pedagogy, and curricular alignment creates a classroom and campus climate that fosters trust in the educational process.[37] That trust does not eliminate conflicts or resistance, but it can mitigate some of the harmful tensions and build a sense of belonging among all students.[38] President Thomas Parham of CSU–Dominguez Hills explains:

> *The fundamental part for me is trust. Do you as a student trust that what I'm about to do in the classroom is the best I can bring to the table? Do you trust that I'm going to create a wholesome environment that allows students to both interrogate the ideas that I bring forward as well as engage in respectful exchange with each other as they agree and disagree? The best kind of teaching happens in those kinds of climates—where students don't feel like they are so robotic that all they have to do is take in information and regurgitate it back, but rather are synthesizing information, are interrogating concepts and constructs, and are engaging alone and together in learning that matters.*

Students in a relationship-rich classroom can navigate, and sometimes even flourish in, conflicts when they arise in the course. Kathleen Fitzpatrick calls this capacity "generous thinking"—the ability not only to articulate and value your own perspectives but also "to care for the quite different concerns of others."[39]

From One to Many Classrooms

Individual faculty can be highly effective in their own courses, but a shared faculty commitment to relational teaching multiplies the number and percentage of students who benefit from relationship-rich classroom experiences. The composition program at California State University–Dominguez Hills illustrates the power of faculty working together. A common assignment in the composition program prompts students to write about their personal experiences with writing and reading, a topic that not only has educational value for students but also provides faculty with insights into students' goals and educational experiences in ways that enable student-faculty relationships to flourish.[40] As Tim Chin, professor and chair of the English department, explains, "relationships and mentoring are embedded in our curricular and pedagogical model, right from the start of the first composition class students take here." Students at Dominguez Hills quickly come to value and to expect strong relationships with peers and faculty across the curriculum. This expectation fosters a "generative culture" of learning and teaching throughout the institution.[41]

The importance of faculty working together within departments and across campus cannot be emphasized enough. Uma Swamy, a chemistry professor at Florida International University, recalls that "when we first started using active learning and peer pedagogies in my classroom, I was pretty much the only person doing it. Everybody looked at me as an oddity. Then other faculty started doing the same thing, and soon students began advocating for active learning in all of their courses." Mary Deane Sorcinelli, a leading scholar of faculty development, reinforces Swamy's experience: "You have to root this work in the faculty culture for it to be successful. What often happens is that faculty begin building relationships with peers to talk about teaching, and that adds to their own confidence and skills, which encourages them not only to continue to work on their own teaching but also to expand the network of colleagues who are doing the same thing."

The power of a culture that develops relationship-rich classrooms is inspiring, even transformational. Tekla Nicholas at Florida International describes how sustained faculty collaboration to improve large courses through relational pedagogies has "dramatically improved student success. Thousands more students are passing their Gateway courses, and when that happens they are more likely to graduate, so their lives are changed—and their families and our communities are changed. The impact of this classroom work is enormous."

Chapter Five

Rich Relationships Everywhere

I learned to be more self-aware and more confident through peer mentoring and through working with the Student Success Mentors program, especially because everyone in this program pushes me. People here see stuff in me that I don't see myself. When I second-guess my ability to do something, my supervisor, Ellen Quish, will say, "Peta, what are you talking about? You're great at that," or "You should work on this." When I'm struggling, I remember Ellen told me I'm awesome. So I'm awesome.

—Peta-Gaye Dixon, LaGuardia Community College

Anne Browning directs the Resilience Lab at the University of Washington. The lab connects staff, students, and faculty on all three UW campuses to facilitate research and programming on resilience and well-being within individuals, communities, and the institution. When the lab began in 2015, Browning related, "We had very few dollars but many people who were invested in our mission." Some early partners came from undergraduate academic affairs initiatives on mentoring and student support. Others were from student affairs programs that focus on well-being, leadership development, and racial, gender, and sexual identities. Others were researchers in medicine, psychology, and other fields, and still others were faculty who sought to cultivate resilience in their classrooms. The lab brings these diverse partners together, challenging the siloed culture that is typical at large and complex universities. Browning says the lab had to learn to "color outside the lines" in ways that "may not get evaluated or supported" within traditional structures. Yet the commitment from people and programs across the institution allows the lab to use an infusion model to do meaningful work in classrooms, student organizations, research labs, mentoring initiatives, and elsewhere so that it quickly became "hard for students to go through the institution without being touched by folks who were thinking seriously about resilience and well-being."

Relationships in college follow this same pattern, rarely "coloring inside the lines" of a single course or program. Instead, peer and faculty interactions spill out of the classroom, extending academic discussions into hallways, coffee shops, and social media. Similarly, relationships and conversations that begin in a student club, on a sports field, or in a staff member's office have ripples that may touch every corner of the campus.

This chapter profiles a range of programs and practices that demonstrate the dynamic power of relationships and the importance of relentless welcome, inspired learning, webs of connections, and meaningful, big questions. Some of the programs here are relatively new; others have been around for decades. Some began with a sustained institutional commitment and others at first had a single champion on campus. These examples highlight the significance of four familiar yet essential themes about relationship-rich experiences in college:

1. Student leadership is a force multiplier.
2. Individual and small-scale initiatives can take root and spread.
3. Technology and data can facilitate relationship building.
4. Broadening access to relationship-rich experiences means rethinking basic structures.

The programs featured in this chapter contribute to a dynamic ecosystem of relationships on their campuses. When an institution aligns its campus culture, classroom practices, student life intiatives, advisement system, assessment plans, reward structures, technological infrastructure, and other programming with student needs positioned at the center, an "interconnected safety net emerges, and students will sense that someone has their back all the time," affirms Donna Linderman of the Accelerated Study in Associate Programs (ASAP). That is essential because, as Timothy Eatman from Rutgers-Newark says, "Any student who is able to develop healthy and inspiring relationships with faculty or other folks on campus will thrive."

Student Leadership Is a Force Multiplier

Undergraduate students can and should be active agents of and leaders in relational practices on campus, in roles such as learning assistants, consultants to faculty, peer advisors, and peer instructors. To effectively and ethically take on these responsibilities, students require careful mentoring and training, often involving seminars that challenge them to develop their capacities to be metacognitive, reflective, and empathetic. Oftentimes these roles provide compensation for students, which delivers the triple benefit of assisting with college expenses, developing valuable professional skills, and more deeply engaging them on campus—especially important for commuting and high-financial need students. The Gateway Project at Florida International University, the Students as Learners and Teachers program (SaLT) at Bryn Mawr and Haverford colleges, peer mentoring at LaGuardia Community College, and the First-Year Interest Group initiative at the University of Washington are illustrations of student leadership in relationship-rich education.

Deepening Relationships through Learning and Course Assistants

Over the past decade, Florida International University has achieved a greater than 40 percent improvement in pass rates in first-year core courses through the Gateway Project. Central to the success of the Gateway Project at this research-intensive and Hispanic-serving institution is a faculty commitment to redesign classes to focus on active pedagogies and to integrate student learning assistants into all aspects of a course. This commitment requires faculty to reconceive their roles as teachers. Senior lecturer in chemistry Uma Swamy "transformed" her lecture-heavy teaching by, first, rejecting the idea that high DFW grade rates in introductory chemistry had to be the norm and, second, changing her teaching practices. Before the Gateway Project, Swamy admits in a disarmingly honest way, "I would stand in front of the class talking my head off." Today, her teaching is centered on substantive small group work facilitated by undergraduate learning assistants: "I now have many chances to observe and interact with my students." These interactions and the data from the Gateway Project have taught Swamy these lessons: "Many of my students do not know how to learn when they come to my class, so I now teach them chemistry in ways that they learn the material and also pick up the skills that will help them succeed more generally in college."

Learning assistants (LAs) are key to the success of transformed courses across the Gateway Project. FIU professor of physics Laird Kramer describes the basic functions of the learning assistant as working inside a classroom to support and encourage student learning, most often in the setting of a small group. To be effective in the classroom, LAs partner with faculty in preparing classroom strategies and activities and also participate in a seminar designed for learning assistants. This LA course focuses on metacognition and discipline-appropriate learning strategies, such as understanding the difference between asking open and closed questions, that will allow the LAs to help their peers learn. FIU adapted its LA program from groundbreaking work done by scholars and students at the University of Colorado–Boulder[1] and the Learning Assistant Alliance.[2]

Danette Barber, coordinator of Nevada State College's course assistant program (a model similar to learning assistants), stresses that these programs help students forge peer learning networks in the classroom: "This is a prime opportunity for building relationships—helping students realize that course assistants are a resource for them and that they can be trusted." These networks serve many purposes, but perhaps the most significant is that they create a more comfortable space for students to express their struggles and confusion in the course. FIU's Kramer notes, "It's very easy to lecture for an hour, ask if there are any questions at the end of class, and then, if you get no questions, to assume everything is perfect. But learning assistants are picking up questions and comments from students that faculty are not aware of, because faculty can't be in everyone's head at the same time."

In addition to supporting learning inside the classroom, many FIU learning assistants also meet one-on-one or with small groups of students outside class during office hours. LA Rosa Espinal recalls that a student spoke to her outside class one day to confide she was thinking of dropping an anatomy class because of a poor grade on the first exam. Espinal listened to the student, and then, she recalls, "I took out my notebook from when I was in anatomy as a student. I showed her my notebook and talked with her about how I learned—taking notes, reviewing videos, rereading my notes. She seemed to be inspired and said to me, 'How about if I try this?' And she got a better grade for the next exam!" Conversations like that one are the foundation of the success of FIU's Gateway Project.

Both FIU's Kramer and Nevada State's Barber stress that some of their best LAs do not have 4.0 grade point averages. Indeed, LAs who "stumbled and recovered" early in their college careers bring a great deal of authenticity to a learning assistant role, according to Barber, and inspire confidence in their peers: *If they could do it, so could I.* A large and diverse group of students at any campus could become learning assistants, expanding the web of educational relationships available to all students—and also empowering students to take on additional leadership roles on campus.

Peer Mentoring

LaGuardia Community College is a leader in leveraging the power of peer mentoring programs to bring relationship-rich education to scale. LaGuardia's programs—Peer Advisor Academy, Student Success Mentors, Student Technology Mentors, Peer Health Educators, Crear Futuros Mentors, and Black Male Empowerment Cooperative Mentors—provide an impressive backbone of student support. Despite LaGuardia's large and diverse student body and the fact that all of its students commute, students describe the sense of belonging that peer mentoring programs promote across campus for cohorts of students. Andrew Espinoza says that his peers at LaGuardia are "open to help" and that "You can go anywhere on campus and find a friend." Ashley Mangual, a Crear Futuros mentor, echoes this view: "I would say that despite the negative connotation that 'community college' gives, this place is absolutely a community. I have been to a couple of different colleges, and I would daresay that many colleges lack that community aspect. Here at LaGuardia, that is not the case." Creating a vibrant sense of community among students at a large, urban, commuting campus is no small feat, and student leadership in peer mentoring programs is key to building those connections.

LaGuardia's students are more diverse than the college's faculty and staff, as is the case at most institutions,[3] so a student looking for support from or a connection with someone who shares an ethnic, racial, gender, sexual, language, or other identity is likely to find those people through a peer program or student organization on campus. Anthony Mota, a student and mentor in Crear Futuros, emphasizes that trained peers can "give someone the platform for them to just be themselves in a nonjudgmental space. That can be really hard. It's important to just listen to their story because everybody's story here is different." Scholars echo Mota's point, stressing the importance of supports, allies, and kinship networks for individuals and groups on campus such as LGBTQIA students.[4]

LaGuardia's mentoring programs also build on the specialized expertise that some students bring to campus and that faculty and staff may lack. A founder of the technology mentor program observes:

> One of the unique things about our mentoring programs is that the student mentors are able to make and extend connections not only student to student, but also student to faculty and staff. This helps make them more engaged with the whole college community. One of the unique aspects of our student technology mentors is that our students started to see faculty and staff as people with the same concerns and learning issues that the rest of us have. It became a mutual learning experience for both our peer mentors, in this case our student technology mentors, and our faculty and staff.

This view of LaGuardia as a community of learners is made possible by the expertise student peer mentors demonstrate, moving beyond the traditional paradigm of undergraduates as those who receive of knowledge and assistance in higher education.

In addition to these benefits to other students, to faculty and staff, and to institutions, the experience can contribute to self-discovery. Ashley Mangual reflects:

I want to talk about peer relationship building in a way that is not so conventional or clear-cut. It's a space to be wrong. And it's a space to confront others and to have others confront you—and to be provided that space for growing and understanding yourself. For me, that is the power of these mentoring programs. They give you an opportunity to look in the mirror through the eyes of people around you so that you learn very deeply both about your flaws and what's good about you. It also gives you the space to practice how to do it all better.

This kind of personal development can be a profound outcome for all students in peer mentoring relationships.

The opportunities to learn, contribute, connect, and grow that peer mentors describe are possible because they receive significant support and training as they adopt and develop in the role. Sometimes, this involves understanding how to triage a student to someone who can offer special expertise, such as psychological counseling, that extends beyond a peer mentor's capabilities. More broadly, peer mentors like Ahsan Bahar value the practical learning gained from participation in these programs: "The Peer Advisor Academy gave us the opportunity to attend different professional development meetings and trainings. This is a win-win, because not only was I able to change students' lives by helping them build positive motivation, but at the same time I was driving myself to be at the level I want to be at."

Students as Learners and Teachers

The Students as Learners and Teachers program at Bryn Mawr College and Haverford College is a faculty development intiative that also aims to empower students to be "active agents of their own learning," according to Alison Cook-Sather, the Mary Katharine Woodworth Professor of Education at Bryn Mawr College and director of the Teaching and Learning Institute at Bryn Mawr and Haverford. The heart of the program is a partnership between faculty (often, but not always, new faculty members) joining either institution and carefully selected and trained student consultants.[5] While SaLT students are, by design, not majors in their faculty partner's discipline, they are both skilled consultants and experienced students who each week observe class and then meet one-on-one with their partners to discuss the course. Consultants benefit from a seminar, facilitated by Cook-Sather, which focuses on how to offer support and affirmation while also making suggestions about the pedagogical practices they observe:

> The explicit goal of the partnership is to create a space within which faculty can reflect on their teaching and articulate their pedagogical commitments in ways they might not otherwise be invited or have the opportunity to do. This allows them to assess their assumptions and to critically consider their classroom practices in ways that are beneficial not only for themselves but also for the students in their courses. The aim is also to support faculty in doing this reflection in a nonthreatening collegial relationship, but with a student, not with a fellow faculty member, because especially in smaller institutions, faculty may feel vulnerable or threatened in these types of conversations with other faculty. Another, and maybe more subversive, goal is to reposition students in their own education from being those who receive knowledge and are told what they need to understand to being active participants in a dialogue about teaching and learning. Because once students are in that kind of dialogue with faculty, they can never go back.

These conversations often lead faculty to be more aware of and transparent about their teaching. Katharine Bancroft, a student consultant from Haverford College, reports, "I have spent a lot of my time with my faculty partner saying, 'I think this will be a lot easier if you just remind the students why you are doing this at the beginning of class before you do it.'" Cook-Sather adds that one of her favorite stories "is about a faculty member who added one key word to his teaching repertoire: *because*." SaLT gives faculty the gifts of time and a trusted student consultant to help them to observe, reflect on, and make changes in their teaching practice.

SaLT student consultants find that their experiences as consultants make them more empathetic and skillful students who are more appreciative of the complexities of classroom dynamics. Bryn Mawr alumna Melanie Bahti explains, "The experience helped me not have my gut reaction to things that happened in the classroom be accusatory or frustrated but to try and understand where those things were coming from and to see everybody in those situations as human." While conducting a midsemester feedback session for her faculty partner, Haverford student consultant Marley Asplundh noticed "how half the class really believes strongly that something helps them learn and half the class feels very strongly that the same thing inhibits their learning. That was a real eye-opening experience about how it is to be a professor accommodating a lot of different individual needs and preferences." Consultant Amaka Eze of Bryn Mawr sums up the experience: "We are privileged to have this very intimate view of what happens behind the scenes with professors, not just in the logistics and the tedium of helping them format a syllabus or plan an activity for class but also in the entire network of responsibilities, associations, and affiliations the professor is always navigating and negotiating."

Faculty report gaining profound insights about their teaching experiences through conversations with their consultants that prompt them to alter how they see their classrooms and students. Theresa Tensuan, associate dean of the college and dean of diversity, access, and community engagement at Haverford recalls that she thought a class discussion in one class period was lively but that it dragged in the next class. Her consultant disagreed:

Zanny told me the first conversation struck her as disoriented but that the second conversation was great because people were building on each other's ideas. So a couple of things came out specifically in terms of pedagogical shifts. I started asking more simple prompts. I love asking multilayered, seventeen-part questions but realized this was not helpful. And I gave three minutes for people to jot down a response—a really simple intervention—but it really made a difference in terms of how deeply people were engaged, rather than the "popcorn effect," which I find I get a lot of energy from.

Conversations like the ones Tensuan describes can be challenging for faculty, who often feel vulnerable as they open their teaching to critical feedback from student consultants, however thoughtful and supportive. As consultant Asplundh observes, "I think for faculty to really buy into this process it takes a big dose of humility and understanding. It also takes a lot of trust in building a relationship." The benefits of the risk and time invested in this partnership, however, can be profound. Andrea Lommen, a professor of physics and astronomy at Haverford College, explains,

My consultant Paul gave me someone to debrief with. When it's just me talking to myself in my office, I will get mired in the trees rather than see the forest. I'll think about the equations my students need to know and forget about the bigger questions about teaching and learning that I have been working on over the last fifteen years. It's taken me a while to realize that I need to say things to students like, "You're doing really well" and "You have learned a lot" and "You don't realize how much you have learned because I just keep throwing these new, really hard things at you."

Besides supporting faculty to enhance their teaching, SaLT also has long-term value for the student consultants. Former Bryn Mawr consultant Maeve O'Hara, now a teacher in the Philadelphia public schools, notes, "What strikes me to this day is that SaLT somehow really gave us voice." The sense of agency students gain as consultants helps them to have courage and confidence in other contexts, including professional settings after they graduate. O'Hara says, "In my current teaching job over the last four years, some of my colleagues don't know how to handle me. I ask questions. I am not afraid of turning things upside down and asking, 'What if this were totally different?'"

SaLT partnerships, and the student consultants in particular, influence both the classroom and the institutional cultures at Bryn Mawr and Haverford in subtle but important ways. SaLT's existence and the consultants' presence in scores of classrooms each year are tangible symbols that teaching is a valued activity and that faculty want to improve, are open to feedback, and care deeply about student learning—and that relationships between students and faculty matter a great deal. Those are the pillars of a generative and relationship-rich culture of teaching and learning, and students are crucial actors in creating and nurturing that culture.

Freshman Interest Groups

How do you create community in the incoming first-year class at a huge research university like the University of Washington? Part of the answer to that question is the First-Year Interest Groups (FIGs) seminar program, which is more than thirty years old and has enrolled hundreds of thousands of students in its history, according to Carlos Guillen, associate director of first-year programs. The heart of the FIGs program is the peer educator, or FIGs leader, who is independently responsible for teaching the seminars. FIGs leaders are taught to develop lesson plans and class activities and "to really build community within their FIG," according to Guillen. FIG seminars are often clustered with general education classes, so the twenty-five students in a FIG seminar might also be co-enrolled in a biology class and an English class.

Max Chan, a junior FIGs leader, recalled his own experience as a first-year student at UW. His FIG seminar required a community research project, an opportunity for small groups of four or five students to identify a neighborhood in Seattle and "explore it, check out the landmarks, architecture, local history, demographics, art, and culture." Chan adds, "I got to explore places I hadn't been yet and it was great to form connections and get to know where I live." He also remembers the "light pressure" his FIGs experience gave him at the beginning of his first year to not only find social friends just like himself but also seek out peers and community members who would cause him to stretch and grow.

Another FIGs activity, the Projecting Forward Project, asks students to go into the community to conduct informational interviews with people in their intended careers or academic fields of study. Chan, who plans a career in professional sports, believes that the experience of speaking to people in organizations like the Seattle Mariners, the Seattle Seahawks, and UW athletics was useful in preparing him for internship interviews.

FIGs leaders have some latitude to design curriculum (only 60 percent of the FIGs curriculum is fixed); they gain experience in lesson planning, leading seminars, and advising students. FIGs leader Marium Khan reports, "One of my proudest moments as a FIGs leader was watching students build connections with one another." FIGs leaders value their first experiences in teaching. Max Chan notes, "Not a lot of college students get this experience. You are trying to find that balance between being their friend, being someone they can come to for support, but also being their instructor. You are in an authoritative role and you have power, and part of being a FIGs leader is having to juggle both sides." Marium Khan reflected that she has "a lot more respect for what my instructors do" following her own experiences as a first-time teacher, such as facing awkward silence after posing a question.

FIGs are light-touch, relationship-rich experiences that can involve thousands of students each year. They also align with a core need and desire of first-year students to make friends and develop a sense of belonging on a very big campus. And FIGs—along with learning assistants, peer mentors, and student pedagogical consultants—illustrate the potential of students to be leaders of relational education.

Individual and Small-Scale Initiatives Can Take Root and Spread

College and university faculty and staff, through their own efforts, can create meaningful and exemplary practices that foster relationships on campus. Simple but important decisions range from holding office hours in places that are welcoming to students to deliberately engaging students when walking in the hallways or across campus. We profile the work of Gretchen McKay with the football team at McDaniel College; Tom Daniels' mentoring a range of protégés in his research laboratory at the University of Washington; the Conversation Center at the University of Iowa, which helps students become more practiced in the art of conversation; and Chancellor Harold Martin's efforts to foster a relationship-rich culture at North Carolina A&T State University.

Deepening Relationships through Mentoring Student Athletes

Gretchen McKay is professor of art history at McDaniel College and a faculty mentor to the football team. For her first decade on the McDaniel faculty, she had no relationship with the team beyond teaching players in some of her courses. Conversations with those students sparked her interest, so she began attending some games and practices. "I'm a very curious person, as most scholars are, and I just wanted to know more about what was happening with these students." What she discovered was revealing and blossomed into her taking on the role of faculty advisor to the team and mentor to many of the players, even those she does not teach in her courses.

Before she reached out to the team, she relates, football student-athletes "didn't see me as connecting to their lives other than as being their art history professor. Now, they recognize that I see them also in terms of their sport, which is very important to their identity. And that opens the door for them to feel like they can talk to me about more than school and registration and classes." Indeed, McKay has come to know some of these student-athletes in much more depth. One African American student described "feeling unwelcome on the campus." She listened to him and then helped him to "craft a program to build his sense of belonging while also improving his grade point average." Another student-athlete confided in her about his struggles with depression, "something I have discovered male athletes do not like to admit and are terrified their coaches will find out." She helped him to find appropriate treatment and counseling, and he "really turned his life around."

McKay emphasizes that her role involves more listening than anything else: "Oftentimes they are not really looking for somebody to solve their problem. They are looking for somebody who will just say, 'I see you and I hear you.'" As she listens, she also learns about the common challenges these men face as both students and athletes on campus, and she has become an advocate for institutional change. She put the issue of bursar holds on the faculty meeting agenda because she heard multiple stories of student-athletes being blocked from class registration because they had small outstanding bills owed to the college. McKay's institution now has significantly raised the baseline amount for a bursar hold on registrations, demonstrating to football players that she—and the college—really listen to student concerns.

She also has changed her art history pedagogy because of her experience watching active young men practice and play football.[6]

"I've developed this tagline of 'active learning for active students.'" After watching her players "never stop moving on the
field, all I could think about was that sitting in class for ninety
minutes listening to someone talk must be torture." Before that
realization, McKay had employed active learning strategies "here
and there—in pockets." She decided to incorporate active learning in every class period of each of her courses, and soon she began experimenting with Reacting to the Past immersive role-
playing games that are set at crucial moments in the past.[7] "I use
a Reacting game every course. Football players are astounding in
Reacting. One said, 'It was like I wasn't here at McDaniel. I was
in this war council in 1148 and forgot that these were my classmates. We were the characters you assigned to us.'"

McKay's leadership in building relationships with student-
athletes on the football team has spurred the college's athletics
department to identify faculty mentors for every sport. Considering that McKay began teaching at a small college "to have
deeper conversations with students than [she] could have at a
much bigger institution," her perhaps unlikely marriage of art
history and football have indeed made significant student-
faculty relationships possible at McDaniel College.

Research Mentoring Constellations

While the undergraduate research model of a single faculty
member mentoring a student one-on-one is well known, some
faculty create research mentoring teams to foster relationships;
these might include undergraduates from all class years, graduate students, postdoctoral students, and faculty. Amy Overman,
a psychology professor at Elon, has carefully documented the
importance of constructing a shared vision in these group mentoring arrangements as well as opportunities to form interlocking projects and communities within a research group.[8] Brad

Johnson of the United States Naval Academy uses the term *research vertical team* to describe this approach:

> *You meet every couple of weeks for a couple of hours to talk about your research and what the students are doing in their capstone projects, and that often leads to a great productive team that can co-author together. But there's this inherent mentoring quality that develops where people are checking in with each other between meetings. This is a great way to build mentoring constellations. I can be there for the formal meetings as a faculty member and provide the primary mentorship, but all of the lateral peer relationships also develop—the more senior students in the group began to take on more supervisory responsibility for the work of the more junior students. So the more senior students under your supervision practice role modeling and mentoring.*

Because faculty expert guidance is essential for student learning, this approach has the potential to multiply the positive outcomes of undergraduate research mentoring experiences as long as faculty remain an integral part of the team.[9] Ed Taylor, vice provost and dean of undergraduate academic affairs at the University of Washington, has witnessed a powerful example of a large faculty-led research team that includes many undergraduates and even a high school student. This research group is headed by a distinguished scholar, Tom Daniels, who holds the Joan and Richard Komen Endowed Chair in the Department of Biology at UW:[10]

> *Tom is a MacArthur winner in biology and neuroscience. He's also won a distinguished teaching award and he's a brilliant researcher—the control and dynamics of movement in biology, the flight of insects and other animals. His lab is such an interesting space because of the constellation of his benches there. I remember when he was giving me a tour. Here's his own bench. He's got a bench for a postdoc; he's got a*

bench for tenure-line faculty and one for graduate students. He has benches for undergraduate students who are all sitting beside each other. I happened to visit last summer and he had a high school student sitting next to him. So here you see an ecosystem of students learning with each other. And he was telling me about each student and who sat at what bench and what they were learning and what they were doing, and he was talking to me about their social-emotional development as well, because he creates space where students can come in at any time they need and have a time to be present with each other and to learn together. He's staying true to his role here, which is to be a scholar, but also leads in mentoring. He doesn't pretend to be the kind of faculty member who is going to meet you in the bar and sit with you for hours and talk about the meaning of life. But if you become one of his students, of which there have been many, he has very carefully stewarded you into the process of scientific research and the profession. It's a lovely thing to see.

Research laboratories such as Tom Daniels' may be the home of some of the most relationship-rich experiences on any campus, as well as the most academically rigorous. By working with research teams rather than one-on-one with students, faculty taking this approach have the potential to bring many undergradutes into the community of scholars.

Deepening Relationships through Conversations

Ben Hassman, director of the Conversation Center at the University of Iowa, shepherds an innovative program designed to promote informal and intercultural student-facilitated conversation on campus.[11] The heart of the program, which is modeled on writing center pedagogy, is a course, The Conversation Practicum, that prepares undergraduate student consultants to learn about intercultural communication and to develop their skills in conversation. This foundation prepares student consultants to "offer ten weeks of one-one-one conversation with anybody who walks through the door" of the Conversation Center. Many clients are international students who want to practice their English, but the center serves a diverse range of people, including "first-generation students and shy students and students who are lonely or who don't feel as connected as they want to. Many of our clients just want someone to talk with and don't know where to go or how to build connections with their peers, so they come to us. And we know these kinds of interactions are important to a student's sense of belonging in the university community."

Alexa Oleson, once a very shy person, believed she had been "transformed" by becoming a trained consultant at the Conversation Center:

> I took the practicum in the spring of my first year. I was really bad at talking to people, especially strangers. I would just freeze up. Even though I am not first generation I didn't come to campus expecting to be connected. I live off campus. I didn't want to join any organizations. I just wanted to go to class and leave. But one of my professors really pushed the Conversation Practicum to me. So I decided to take it to better my own personal speaking skills, and it changed my experience on campus because I really did get involved.

Three essential factors enabled Oleson to have this profound learning experience. First, an astute professor in the classroom made an important observation and recommendation. Second, the Conversation Practicum offered training, support, and opportunity for practice in the art of conversation. Third, she was brave enough to stretch herself to develop new skills and confidence. Her initial conversation as a student consultant demonstrates her tenacity and ability to push through her initial fears:

> In my very first Conversation Center appointment, I went in and was so nervous I was shaking. I felt I had a panic attack coming on. I was sitting

there and this person walks up and sits across from me and he looks ten times as nervous as I do. He literally has sweat beading on his forehead and he just looked so nervous. But his anxiety kind of helped me calm down because I realized that we were both in the same position where we were so afraid to talk to each other. So you just calm down and ground yourself. It's just a conversation.

Oleson saw her own vulnerability in the face of another student and yet discovered the courage to reach out and help, a first step toward becoming a more involved student and skilled relationship builder on campus. Her story illustrates the importance both of students taking the initiative to build relationships and of institutions providing a relationship-rich environment with a constellation of opportunities for meaningful connections. For students like Oleson, the Conversation Center is not just one office on a massive campus like the University of Iowa; it is a place of powerful growth and belonging.

Creative Office Hours

Professor Shaun Vecera of the Department of Psychological and Brain Sciences at the University of Iowa struggled for years to get his students to come to his office to meet with him. Now he takes his office hours to his students:

One of the things that I do with my office hours is to hold them in one of the residence halls, and I actually get really very good foot traffic because of that. I don't think students ever want to come alone for one-on-one conversation, particularly if they have to navigate the maze of offices in an unfamiliar building. So I encourage them to come in groups, and we meet in a conference room in a prominent place in the residence hall—a place that's comfortable for them. They come in with their roommate or they come in with someone that they've been studying with who is in their discussion section, and sometimes they come on their own. And there are a lot of very informal relationships that seem to evolve in my "conference room hours" just by having this structure where they can more easily access both me and peers who are also in the class.

Bryan Dewsbury, a biologist at the University of Rhode Island, has also moved his office hours to a student residence hall and has renamed them "student hours" to clarify their purpose, since many of his students come to campus believing that "office hours" are time for faculty to be in their offices getting their own work done and that students will be a bother! Dewsbury finds:

Some of my most robust conversations happen during student hours, which I hold in the dorms because it's a bigger room and more space and more people can come. In the student hours, it's not me just reteaching them. I ask different students to take the lead in teaching different things. Somebody goes to the white board, and others encourage and support and critique what they're doing on the board. And I invariably have students do a lot of work in small groups within "student hours" because sometimes there's quite a crowd. I'll also stop and have an individual conversation when a student wants or needs that; most times it's about the subject we are studying, but I'll use it as a jumping-off point to ask them about their degree plans and potential careers.

Dewsbury's and Vecera's reinvention of office hours is a powerful example of how individual faculty can creatively act to yield relationship-rich results for many of their students.

Prioritizing Time for Student Conversations

Chancellor Harold L. Martin Sr. presides over North Carolina Agricultural and Technical State University (A&T) not only with a deep appreciation of the institution's storied history as one of the eminent Historically Black Colleges and Universities (HBCUs) but also with a farsighted strategy of what is required to shape A&T's future as one of his state's leading universities and STEM research centers. A significant aspect of his approach is to recruit a more diverse student body "who could go anywhere they want to go to college," welcoming more international students, Latinx students, white students, and first-generation students to A&T's vibrant campus.

An A&T alumnus himself, Martin is committed to sustaining a culture that values student engagement and close relationships between students and faculty and staff—longtime trademarks of A&T and other HBCUs.[12] "I think this begins with my own experience as a student coming from a low-income family with parents who were not college going," Martin said. "Relationships with my faculty and administrators as an undergraduate student shaped my thinking about my future and gave me the confidence to look beyond the limits I had set for myself to go on and earn a PhD and to think about higher education as a career."

Martin's calendar reflects his commitment to student relationships, and he understands the power of his personal example. He regularly sets aside time to meet individually with students in half-hour intervals in his office to discuss their aspirations and what A&T is doing to help fulfill them. The chancellor and his spouse also host twenty dinners each year at their residence, inviting forty students to each dinner for conversation and informal games. A&T provides funding to academic deans to offer similar programs in their homes, as well as for faculty and staff to engage with students over lunch or coffee in the student center. "This is the relational culture we nurture on this campus," explains Martin.

He also makes it a practice to walk rather than drive across campus, and his staff build in time for him to interact with students along the way. He says that students and alumni regularly tell him, "You may not remember this, but we bumped into each other on campus one day, and you made a big difference through that conversation." Chancellor Martin's commitment to knowing and interacting with his students is tone setting on the A&T campus and a key element of maintaining his institution's relationship-rich culture.

Technology and Data Can Facilitate Relationship Building

Technology-based innovations can support faculty and staff in their advising and mentoring roles by leveraging the power of data, allowing them to concentrate on higher-order concerns with students rather than on routine work. Examples include the use of simple email templates at Brown University that can be customized by faculty to facilitate purposeful communications with their advisees; the Excelling@Iowa program at the University of Iowa, a predictive analytics program that identifies and supports first-year students who are struggling; and the Elon Experiences Transcript at Elon University, which assists advisors in tracking student participation in high-impact practices.

Staying in Touch

Rashid Zia knows how challenging it can be for busy faculty to stay in regular touch with their undergraduate advisees. He also knows that advising can be a "transactional or a transformational process, depending on the nature of the relationship." As dean of the college at Brown University, Zia oversees advising and the broader undergraduate experience. He has adapted tools he used to communicate with his students from his own time as an engineering faculty member at Brown to support strong student-advisor relationships.

Throughout the academic year at key advising opportunities, Zia and his colleagues send all faculty advisors an email designed to be adapted and sent by faculty to their advisees, at their discretion. These communications keep advisors updated about important deadlines, suggest prompts they might use to encourage students to join clubs and find peers with similar interests, and identify other campus resources for student support. The emails to faculty also include hyperlinks that automatically create draft messages to advisees (including the advisee's preferred name and contact information) that can be easily edited to add personalized messages from faculty advisors. Zia has found that these emails have been "surprisingly successful at helping to connect faculty and students" by making it easy for advisors to send timely messages to students. Most advisors send a handful of them each semester. The customized messages also spark in-person follow-up conversations that build stronger, more meaningful relationships between students and their advisors.

Predictive Analytics and Relationship Building

Danielle Martinez, associate director of academic support and retention at the University of Iowa, describes Excelling@Iowa as "our homegrown student success platform." This system integrates many of the common early-alert functions that institutions use to monitor and support first-year students with features that encourage relationship building. Excelling@Iowa surveys students three to five weeks into the semester, with their responses used as one data point—along with performance data from courses and other factors—to predict who might be having difficulty adjusting to college or be at risk for withdrawal. Careful analysis of the survey results reveals that, as Martinez explains, "some predictive questions have to do with faculty relationships, including (1) How many times have you been to office hours? and (2) How many of your professors know your name?"

The key to Excelling@Iowa is not collecting the data, of course, but getting useful information into the hands of people who will act in ways that will support and engage students. University College, which designed and runs Excelling@Iowa, aims to ensure that every first-year student has at least two formal sources for support on campus to complement the personal networks that students will build on their own through their majors, student clubs and other organizations, and the myriad other opportunities available on campus. For residential students, the resident assistant or hall coordinator is one of those two formal supports. For nonresidential students, including most transfers, faculty and staff volunteers from every part of campus sign up to form relationships with incoming students. A second formal source of support is the academic advisor. People in formal student support roles are given weekly updates on the status of their students, according to Martinez: "Every Monday we send out our predictions update and then also we have strategic points in the semester where we encourage outreach to students." Her office also provides resources such as email and phone script templates to give advisors some tools in preparation for making student contact.

Near the end of the fall semester, University College sponsors a reception for the individuals whom students name in the Excelling survey as their most important supports on campus. The list includes people in formal student support roles, and it also always includes staff in campus dining halls, office assistants, TAs, and others who may not be recognized for—or see themselves as—important relationships for first-year students. This festive event includes remarks by the chancellor or provost underscoring the essential role people across campus and in a wide variety of roles play in helping first-year students feel they belong and can succeed at Iowa.

Experiential Transcripts

Under the leadership of the Division of Student Life and then Vice President for Student Life Smith Jackson, Elon University pioneered the Elon Experiences Transcript in 1994, tracking student engagement in five key practices: global study, internships, leadership, service learning, and undergraduate research. The Elon Experiences Transcript complements the traditional academic transcript, giving academic advisors, prospective employers, and other appropriate parties fuller pictures of students' undergraduate experiences and providing the foundation for discussions around big questions about students' short- and long-term goals.[13] Over the past several years, Rodney Parks, registrar at Elon, has built on this foundation to pioneer other creative ways to use transcripts and data housed in the registrar's and allied offices on campus to strengthen both advising and classroom relationships between students and faculty.

These relationships profoundly shape a student's path through Elon. Parks has analyzed years of institutional data to find that "the average number of experiences for one particular advisor might be six, but another advisor year after year has advisees who pursue from eighteen to twenty experiential learning opportunities." That observation has sparked efforts to better understand how certain advisors work with students in ways that lead students to be passionate about engaged learning. The findings from that research are shaping the way all advisors are trained and supported, so more faculty can employ the effective strategies that their peers have developed to connect with their advisees. The root issue, according to Parks, is to move students away from a mentality of "I'm going to graduate in four years, so I need to check off these boxes" toward an aspiration to make the most of their college years in and out of the classroom. The Elon Experiences Transcript is a good prompt for students and faculty advisors to regularly discuss that broader goal.

Parks and his colleagues also have developed tailored class rolls for certain courses. All Elon undergraduates, for instance, take a capstone seminar before graduation. The focus of these capstones varies based on the expertise of the professor teaching each section, but all share a goal of prompting students to integrate their educational experiences at Elon into a coherent and meaningful whole. The thirty to forty faculty teaching capstones every semester receive reports from the registrar that give them information about their students' academic and experiential learning before they begin the capstones. While that information is available without this report, it is scattered in separate databases that make it impractical for faculty to gather it on their own. The tailored report allows faculty to plan their courses to leverage the learning and experiences students bring with them to the capstone. One humanities faculty member "was stunned that nearly every student in [the capstone] class had taken economics during the completion of their core requirements," so economics colleagues were invited to join certain class conversations to build on the existing relationships and expertise the students brought to the classroom.[14]

Now that faculty and staff across campus have witnessed the power of these capstone class rolls and the experiential transcript, they are coming to Parks with ideas for new ways to use institutional data to develop more meaningful and relational practices with students. Parks recognizes the "potential benefits of having an immense amount of data," but he also worries about ways to safeguard student privacy and ensure equity in the emerging world of data-driven, technology-enabled undergraduate education.[15]

Broadening Access to Relationship-Rich Experiences Means Rethinking Basic Structures

All students should have access to relationship-rich undergraduate experiences, but if relational and high-impact practices are to be truly inclusive, institutions must reexamine basic assumptions to ensure that all students can thrive.[16] Many programs on campuses are rooted in traditional conceptions of college. To explore innovative approaches to access, we profile both the Honors College and the Honors Living-Learning Community (HLLC) at Rutgers University–Newark, one of the most diverse research universities in the United States. The HLLC is a bold new experiment to re-envision what civically engaged honors education can look like, while the Honors College—a more traditional program—employs intensive advising to guarantee that all students, including first-generation students, gain access to research opportunities, international study, and other enriching experiences that will be critical to their success.

Deepening Relationships through Inclusive Honors Frameworks

Honors colleges and honors programs are obvious places to look to find long-established traditions of significant relationships between students and faculty. When you combine academically oriented students, inspiring faculty teachers and mentors, creatively designed courses and curricula, generous scholarships, special honors housing, and more, the odds of incredible outcomes are on your side. Rutgers University–Newark leads the way in thinking imaginatively and effectively about honors education for new majority students through its Honors College and its Honors Living-Learning Community.

Brian Murphy, a history professor and director of the Honors College, tells the story of a student who personifies how Rutgers-Newark is challenging traditional conceptions of honors students and honor education:

> At my first Honors College graduation that I ran when I got here in 2016, we had a student who grew up 10 miles from here who missed the ceremony because he was working a double shift at George's Garage doing a brake job. I get it. You need money, right? And in his case he needed the job because his father is out of work due to disability, and it

was his responsibility to help put food on the table for the family. One way of framing honors education is that it is something that is elitist or exclusive. But that guy who was doing the brake job, there's nothing particularly elite about him, right? He's just a very high performing student who needed access to opportunities that he wouldn't probably have had otherwise. So he had this extra layer of advising helping him to get to where he wanted to go, which was law school.

Indeed, that "extra layer" of advising is key to the ethos of assisting high-performing scholars of the Honors College. Alexandra Torres, a senior majoring in biology with a concentration in neurobiology, references opportunity after opportunity that her Honors College network extended to her, from a first-year colloquium on the philosophy of happiness to an invitation to compete for an internship at the Mena Laboratory of Neural Circuits to being encouraged to apply for study abroad scholarships, which enabled her to pursue research on medieval medicine and complete a thesis on Hildegard of Bingen. She credits Murphy as a steady source of counsel and advice: "I've gone to him so many times and said, 'I don't know what to do. I don't know where to turn with this application. What am I supposed to do with my summer? What do I need to do to become a good candidate?' Because honors is such an intimate setting, Dr. Murphy will clear his schedule to work with his students. I am so grateful to be able to work with someone like that."

Another key part of the Honors College at Rutgers-Newark involves faculty paying attention to helping students reconcile their pursuit of a life of the mind with the pressure they face to graduate and get a job. Murphy explains that on a recent survey, 70 percent of respondents indicated that their primary reason for being in school was to "be a better provider for their family." He credits Chancellor Nancy Cantor for "making an affirmative case for undergraduate education in the liberal arts when very few other people were" as foundational to helping students understand they can avail themselves of the benefits of a liberal education and still "square that up" with the practicality of pursuing a career. Professor of English Sadia Abbas contends that faculty—in and beyond the Honors College—play an essential role in helping first-generation students see beyond the pressures to be upwardly mobile: "They need permission to be intellectual." And that permission is oftentimes not initially granted by families who view education as a means to financial security, which is not a trivial concern. So students need faculty mentors who can advise them as they negotiate this very real tension in their lives.

Chancellor Cantor's vision prompted Rutgers-Newark to pursue another imaginative path for honors education, the Honors Living-Learning Community, an experiment that achieved national attention in its early days in *The New York Times* and on the *PBS NewsHour*.[17] In fundamental ways, the HLLC reconsiders what it means to enter an honors community by emphasizing qualifications for admitted students based on their commitments to social change and becoming leaders and change agents in their local communities, especially Newark. What animates the HLLC experiment are questions like these: What would honors look like if the criteria we used for admission included demonstrated resilience and tenacity? What potential for leadership and community engagement do students demonstrate? What ideas do students have for creating a better world? Student passion for social change is what attracted Joshua Abrego to the HLLC, but it was the intentional "development and teaching us about *how* to make change locally and globally" that has made the HLLC experience so enriching and satisfying for him.

Student Mohamed Farge reinforces the idea of how important webs of relationships are to HLLC students. "The dean told us that the HLLC is about building us to be engines for positive change and that I seemed to fit. But in order to do that, you need a support system." HLLC student Stacy Tyndall notes that relationships, which form the basis of a support system, begin in the interview process and set a tone for students being known and heard within the program: "My capstone, my volunteer work, my internships, and many conversations have taught me to be brave and to be who I am."

Through a public-private partnership, Rutgers-Newark is opening an $81 million five-story signature building to house the diverse students that are selected for participation as well as the dean's office and seminar rooms. Timothy K. Eatman, the inaugural dean of the HLLC, explains "the room styles are commensurate with the types of students we have. We have thirty-five-year-old students. We have seventeen-year-old students. Some of our students have families. We have some formerly incarcerated students. So we are really trying to leverage this notion of what an intergenerational community means."

As an affirmation of the program's promise, the HLLC received a $10 million gift (the largest in the institution's history) to create the Prudential Scholars program for Newark residents and to fund scholarships for HLLC scholars to provide for room, board, and fees. Student Tatyana Harold summarized HLLC's mission as "of Newark and for Newark," reflecting an aspiration that the ideas of excellence and civic leadership can come together in bold and creative new ways by reimagining the purposes and people of traditionally relationship-rich honors education.

* * *

The programs and approaches profiled in this chapter share a commitment to relationship-rich experiences that challenge students to integrate the learning they are doing in the classroom with the experiences they are having on and beyond campus.

This approach is rooted in the assumption, in the words of Alison Cook-Sather of Bryn Mawr, that "students need to be active agents of their own learning." That alone is not enough, however. To reach their potential, students need to be engaged in meaningful conversations with peers, faculty, and staff to help them recognize their own capacities, to provide expert guidance, or to spur them to take action. These long-term mentoring relationships, complemented by timely conversations with "mentors of the moment," are critical in students' educations and lives.

Chapter Six

Mentoring Conversations

My undergraduate research mentor right from the start was really careful about how I thought about science and making sure that my voice was validated and that I was asking questions in lab meetings. She also would carve out time to talk one-on-one about science. She'd ask what I think and really listen to what I said. That's how I learned to develop my science brain.

—Samantha Paskvan, University of Washington

University of Michigan student and peer mentor Brandon Bond took one of his advisee's worries to heart:

> She is a pre-med student and so of course she was worried about completing all of these required classes; however, she really wanted to study abroad and worried she would never be able to do that because of her pre-med requirements. So one day I sat down with her at one of our cafés and pulled out a study abroad program catalog so we could narrow down her top program options. After doing so she was then worried about money, so we made the whole budget for everything, and I suggested some scholarships she should apply for through the university. She eventually had a plan to pay for everything, to study abroad, and to stay in pre-med.

A conversation in a café turned the improbable into the possible, influencing the nature and quality of a student's undergraduate education.

Every day, on every college and university campus, moments like this take place among students, faculty, staff, alumni, and others. Sometimes these conversations are the result of chance encounters on sidewalks. Other times they constitute more formal meetings to discuss specific issues or questions. They might stem from existing relationships or passing acquaintance. However they occur, mentoring conversations have the potential to be consequential moments in the lives of students.

Mentoring in higher education is commonly understood to be a sustained relationship between a scholar and a protégé. The more senior mentor offers expert knowledge and sage advice that makes it possible for the student to eventually enter the community of scholars. To yield life-changing results, this form of mentoring takes time and commitment.[1] One-on-one mentoring is an academic ideal but nearly impossible to scale at the undergraduate level because the sheer quantity of protégés overwhelms the number of available mentors. The math just does not work at most institutions. Fortunately, shorter forms of mentoring interactions—particularly one-on-one or group conversations with peers or faculty or staff members who can ask insightful questions or offer timely advice—have been demonstrated to have powerful outcomes for undergraduates.[2]

Scholars and practitioners use different terminology to describe these kinds of mentoring conversations. Brad Johnson of the United States Naval Academy uses the term *mentor of the moment* to describe an aspect of a healthy culture where meaningful interactions are normal, everyday occurrences:

> *I think it's very powerful in a culture when mentoring is valued and says, "This is a part of who we are and what we do. It's part of our daily activity. It's part of the way we show up to work. It's who we are as a culture." People, including faculty, are empowered to be mentors of the moment to people they encounter who are not their primary advisees. They're the kind of folks who when they walk down the hall or when*

they're walking across campus and they see someone, they're willing to stop and check and ask, How are you doing? What's going on? Even though we only have a few minutes, sometimes in these short interactions, special kinds of wisdom can be passed along, permission can be given, and inspiration can be offered.

Mary Deane Sorcinelli, a leading scholar of faculty development, uses the term *just-in-time mentoring* to describe these interactions. She also underscores that such conversations are good for everyone in higher education, not only students: "Just-in-time mentoring is that moment of conversation where someone directs me to a particular individual I need to talk with or sits down with me and makes one thing particularly clear about what's happening in my classroom right now. It doesn't have to be this long, extensive, three- or four-year commitment for the interaction to be meaningful."

Sean James, director of the Educational Opportunity Program at California State University–Dominguez Hills, employs the term *mentoring on the run* to describe capturing the power of moments in the busy lives of students and student affairs staff, emphasizing that what might seem a casual conversation is actually an opportunity for lasting impact: "'Mentoring on the run' describes those times when you are passing a student and just ask them a simple, pointed question. I think there are a lot of things we can do in those unstructured moments to really help students gain understanding and belonging." Of course, the art in posing such a question is to pause and listen to the response and then take time to offer a comment, a reflection, a bit of tailored advice, a word of encouragement, or a challenging follow-up.

Mentoring conversations, whether sustained over long periods or grabbed "on the run," "just in time," or "of the moment," are much more likely to happen in a culture that values and practices mentoring in many forms and locations throughout the college. Sharon Parks underscores the importance of webs of mentoring programs and networks: "Optimal learning and development depend on access to a mentoring environment, and higher education functions best when there is clear understanding of this critical role: how the academy is composed of multiple mentoring communities, each providing in appropriate and accountable ways the recognition, support, challenge, and inspiration so vital for emerging adult lives."[3]

Members of authentic mentoring communities attend to students' growth and development and act on the idea that relationships are the indispensable building blocks of such communities. Drawing on a longitudinal study of students and alumni at Hamilton College, Daniel Chambliss and Christopher Takacs describe this concept with special clarity:

> Relationships are central to a successful college experience. They are the necessary precondition, the daily motivator, and the most valuable outcome. Therefore, specific human beings matter. A student must have friends, needs good teachers, and benefits from mentors. . . . Mentors, we found, can be invaluable and even life changing. Relationships shape in detail students' experience: what courses they take or majors they declare, whether they play a sport or join an extracurricular activity, whether they gain skills, grow ethically, or learn whatever is offered in various programs. Relationships are important because they raise or suppress the motivation to learn; a good college fosters the relationships that lead to motivation.[4]

The power of mentoring conversations is not reserved for students at small or elite colleges and universities. Randy Bass of Georgetown stresses that "we need to tell the counternarrative that relationships are actually what make *all* of higher education so powerful for *all* students. Whether it's advisors or peer mentors, all of those relationships are at the heart of education, not just elite education." Zaretta Hammond reinforces Bass's assertion by placing "authentic relationships" at the heart of culturally responsive teaching.[5] Indeed, this point is echoed throughout the research on undergraduate education; a recent synthesis from the Stanford Graduate School of Education boldly tells students that if you intentionally focus on learning and community, including seeking out faculty, staff, and peer mentors, you "are more likely to thrive after college."[6]

Laurent Parks Daloz, a scholar of mentoring and higher education, uses the metaphor of a tree to illustrate what a community of mentoring is really all about:

> Ecologists tell us that a tree planted in a clearing of an old forest will grow more successfully than one planted in an open field. The reason, it seems, is that the roots of the forest tree are able to follow the intricate pathways created by former trees and thus embed themselves more deeply. Indeed, over time, the roots of many trees may actually graft themselves to one another, creating an interdependent mat of life hidden beneath the earth's surface. This literally enables the stronger trees to share resources with the weaker so the whole forest becomes healthier. Similarly, we human beings thrive best when we grow in the presence of those who have gone before.[7]

If every student is to put down deep roots in college and to thrive after graduation, then each individual on campus must be conscious of how interconnected we are and the enormous potential we hold when we share with our students our expertise and our own humanity.

Characteristics of Meaningful Mentoring Conversations

From the hundreds of interviews we conducted, along with a critical reading of the relevant scholarship, we have identified five essential characteristics of meaningful mentoring conversations:

1. Mentoring conversations create space for students to be heard and to be human.
2. Mentoring conversations include "nitty-gritty" guidance and knowledge.
3. Mentoring conversations include "warm handoffs" that facilitate yet more relationships.
4. Mentoring conversations are especially important during low moments in students' lives.
5. Mentoring conversations leave legacies.

Each of these characteristics of meaningful mentoring conversations is elaborated upon in the following sections.

Mentoring Conversations Create Space for Students to Be Heard and to Be Human

Kristen Verhey, the A. Kent Christensen Collegiate Professor of Cell and Developmental Biology at the University of Michigan, recalls a mentoring conversation that began with a surprising discovery:

> *Several years ago, in my cell biology research lab, I had as a new undergraduate researcher a young woman from a small town in Michigan who didn't believe in evolution. It took me a couple months to figure that out because the subject didn't come up in the interview process. But because we talk a lot about evolutionary relationships between different proteins, she eventually brought this up. I think it took a lot of courage for her to tell me that she didn't believe in evolution. I had never encountered this before with a student studying biological sciences. I told her that I don't think religion and evolution are mutually exclusive in my view, but I just encouraged her to talk with other people, too. I told her that college is a time for exploring different areas, and this is your opportunity to explore, so ask around and think deeply about your beliefs and your life.*

By taking her student's beliefs seriously, Verhey created a space for this student to wrestle with a fundamental tension she would encounter throughout her education and career in science. Verhey also recognized that she did not need to resolve this tension for the student. Mentors in college do not need to solve every problem or provide every answer to matter in the lives of students. Sometimes students just need to be heard.

Other times, students need more than someone to listen to them, they need faculty or staff to act—to reach out, to advise, to console, to advocate for, or to support them in building relationships and communities (and, as we have suggested elsewhere in the book, to create more welcoming and equitable policies and practices within our institutions). This need is particularly urgent for first-generation and underrepresented students who bring great ambitions to higher education only to experience college as a place of isolation and alienation. Torie Weiston-Serdan, a scholar who focuses on mentoring new majority students, explains:

> Colleges and universities have unique roles to play in critical mentoring processes because marginalized and minoritized students often arrive at these campuses believing that they have somehow moved past many of the challenges they have had with the debilitating structures we've been discussing. They are often shocked and devastated when they discover that they must still work to have their humanity recognized, that inequity is still very entrenched in higher education spaces, that they may have an even harder time acquiring mentors at this level. They have made it through high school and into college, which for most young people is a celebrated stop en route to their dream, but they still require mentoring relationships to help them move to their next levels.[8]

Many of our interviews echoed Weiston-Serdan's insight about the importance of a faculty or staff member, or a trained peer, taking the initiative to recognize and validate a student's full humanity. Arnold Moctezuma, a student at John Jay College (and a LaGuardia Community College graduate), recalls how his own life experiences inform the peer mentor he is today:

> *In the past, when someone tried to offer me their time and their words, I just wasn't open to it. A lot of it had to do with the trauma and conflicts that I had to deal with growing up. Those experiences closed off my mind from receiving help, preventing me from joining the world in the way that I wanted to. I was stuck in my thoughts and in my head. Now I take a look at some of the students that I've mentored and recognize that hesitation, that discomfort that they might be feeling, because I felt that too. So then it becomes a question of, How do I reach this person? because I know what it's like to be there and not know a way out of that mental cycle.*

Moctezuma knows that as a peer mentor he needs to be consistently, sometimes even stubbornly, present for the students he works with at LaGuardia. He cannot wait for each student to ask for help. Some need to know that he can empathize with the discomfort they are feeling before they will be open to meaningful conversations with him, and *he* needs to be the one nudging their peer mentoring relationship in that direction.

Andru Anderson, Posse Scholar and a soon-to-be graduate of Wheaton College in Massachusetts, echoes this point about reaching out to students who might be feeling vulnerable: "I am pro student. I want to see students not only survive but thrive in all their endeavors. I will tell them, especially students of color, you have to learn how to be your own biggest advocate. People aren't mind readers. They don't know what they don't know until you tell them—explicitly tell them. Know that you are an asset to any institution you ultimately decide to attend. They are lucky to have you."

Faculty and staff should learn from Anderson, Moctezuma, and Weiston-Serdan about the need to affirmatively build relationships with all students in our classes and across our campuses. We need to create relationship-rich environments and interactions so all students can thrive.

Supportive, humane relationships also can help students overcome isolation in the world of online learning, where opportunities for spontaneous interactions in the classroom or hallway are absent. Southern New Hampshire University's writing coaches provide personal connections for students who are in fully online courses. Kayleigh Guzel sees these writing coaching interactions as fundamentally about being a human presence in these students' educations: "They are alone in the cloud, essentially. They have discussion boards where they can interact with peers and they have email, but the only voices they actually ever hear are ours and their advisors' when we talk on the phone with them, so we are able to be the human. That's what we do."

Mentoring Conversations Include "Nitty-Gritty" Guidance and Knowledge

Roberta Espinoza studies Latinx students' experiences with education and mentoring. She demonstrates that many students need more than encouragement and listening from mentors; they need practical guidance and expert knowledge.[9] Brad Johnson's research also stresses the importance of moments when experienced mentors can help students "fill in the blanks" about a discipline, college life, or their future careers: "This is what professionalism looks like—the nitty-gritty stuff that you and I take for granted, like what do you wear and what do you say in certain contexts."

This is especially important for students who are the first in their families to negotiate college or to enter particular professions.

Javier Solorzano, program manager in the Office of Multi–Ethnic Student Affairs at the University of Michigan, speaks of his own experience: "A perfect example is myself—first-generation, former undocumented, and low economic status student whose family was deported to Mexico. I had introductory questions that I asked my mentor. These questions ranged from where I should live and how I should pay my rent to what an office hour was. My mentor was able to surface those questions and provide resources and feedback though a natural, meaning-making conversation." Without this vital information, Solorzano may have struggled mightily to earn two degrees from Michigan and to succeed as a professional at the university.

Students often feel more comfortable receiving some types of information from individuals who are not in positions to formally grade or evaluate them. Hyun-Soo Seo of the University of Michigan states, "Allowing for mentees to have a space to let loose and connect with someone who may have a little more experience than them (but isn't the professor) is profoundly important."

Sometimes a mentor's role is not to impart knowledge but to ask guiding questions and to support a student through the process of an unfamiliar task or experience. Meredith Vallee, a writing coach at Southern New Hampshire University, describes this kind of conversation as central to the work she and her colleagues do with students:

> When students are struggling with an assignment, we never say, "This is what your assignment is telling you to do." But we suggest how to analyze and interpret what is being asked and then we help students through the process of creating outlines for assignments all the way through to full drafts, creating things like thesis statements, an organization of ideas, all the way through proofreading and grammar review and comma splices and whatever it is they need. We help them stay on task by paying attention to time management, and we talk with them

about how to conduct research and how to synthesize resources into
their work.

This practical knowledge and coaching is vital to the success of students at Southern New Hampshire and across higher education.[10] Effective mentoring conversations often require people to get their hands dirty when talking about college, career, and life.

Mentoring Conversations Include "Warm Handoffs" That Facilitate Yet More Relationships

No individual can be an expert in everything students might need or want from mentoring conversations. That is one reason students should develop intersecting webs of teachers, mentors, advisors, peers, and others who offer complementary knowledge, expertise, and wisdom. Mentors also need to recognize the limits of their own capacities and the professional boundaries that guide their relationships with students. Fortunately, colleges and universities are brimming with people who can support and challenge students in many different ways.

Adam Kasarda, director of the Student disAbility Resource Center at California State University–Dominguez Hills, emphasizes the importance of the "warm handoff" in mentoring conversations. This term emerges from both behavioral health care and customer service and refers to the act of introducing patients or clients to those who have the special expertise to attend to their needs. Drawing on this approach, Kasarda trains frontline student workers in his office to be expert facilitators in getting students to the resources they need in a manner that assures they will not fall through the cracks. Kasarda's colleague Maruth Figueroa illustrates this simple but powerful principle:

> *I have found over the years working in the area of Student Success, I as*
> *an advisor can say, "Hey, let me walk you to the Learning Center and*
> *let me introduce you to Olivia, who can help you find the support that*

you need." Students are put at ease with that, and it's so much more
likely to result in a lasting connection than just telling a student, "Go
talk to Olivia in the Learning Center."

Kasarda also underscores the importance of personal rapport
to increase the chances that these warm handoffs will happen in
the first place and cautions about overburdening students with
too much information:

The other piece that I've learned over my years is that with my popula-
tion, if I keep pestering them, I push them away. You have to give them
just enough information, just when they need it. Give them the informa-
tion about where the office is, who the contact is, what the process is, the
steps and any documents they may need, and they will come to you when
they are ready. The biggest part is that getting-ready piece, and that's
where rapport is so important. If you have a bad relationship or a bad
start with the student, they're less likely to come back in. If you come at it
from a very friendly, open space, they're going to return much quicker,
ready to get going.

These acts of relationship-building may have only short-term
outcomes, or they may be transformative. Most often, warm
handoffs on campus are low-stakes ways of helping students
connect with tutors, counselors, experts, resources, or peers
who will contribute to their personal and academic success. At
other times, as with Professor Gretchen McKay's "warm handoff" of a student-athlete who struggled with depression (chapter 5), these interactions can be vital for a student's future in and
beyond college. And warm handoffs can also connect students
with potential longer-term mentors who may very well be key
influencers in their lives. Ayanna McConnell from the University of Michigan recalls a first-generation student she had come
to know through a mentoring program who aspired to be a dentist but did not have any professional connections: "My program

has a board member and Michigan alum who is a dentist. I told him a bit about this student, and then I made sure she came to a networking event where I introduced the two of them. They have been in contact ever since, and he has been integral in her career path."

Mentoring Conversations Are Especially Important during Low Moments in Students' Lives

Nearly all students' lives contain low moments such as a failed course, a serious illness, the loss of a parent, the experience of feeling completely alone and adrift, or an honor code violation. Relationships can be especially crucial in those times. One Elon parent illustrated this lesson immediately following commencement in 2016. He walked into the president's office to express his gratitude for his son's education, proudly announcing that his son had accepted a scholarship to attend a prestigious law school. Then he pulled out three checks. The first was a donation in honor of pre-law advisor Chalmers Brumbaugh who had served as a critical coach and mentor to his son. The second was a tribute to his son's senior seminar history professor, Charles Irons, who had challenged his son to stretch further academically than he thought possible. The third honored Dean of Students Jana Lynn Patterson, who, in the words of this parent, "gave my son a kick in the pants during his first year." Apparently this student had engaged in some "knucklehead" behavior during his first semester, and Dean Patterson called him into her office for a conversation about the consequences of his actions and the looming risk to his educational future. When told of the gift in her honor, Patterson recalled, "Yes, I gave him a little 'talking to.' But then I gave him a hug." The father was grateful to Patterson for not letting his son's behavior slide, for issuing a stern warning, and then for expressing faith that his son would make better decisions in the future. That moment, the father believes, was pivotal in his son's academic career and in his life. What could have been a transactional disciplinary matter instead became a moment for mentoring.

As student life leaders know well, mentoring conversations with students at perhaps the lowest moments of their college careers can be particularly powerful. These are times when faculty and staff—and sometimes peers—must reach out to students to help them through crises. These moments often lead to warm handoffs for additional support from counselors or caregivers. Such compassionate conversations can be the beginning of bouncing back and can teach important lessons about resilience and humility.

Mentoring Conversations Leave Legacies

Brad Johnson notes, "People often say that the mentor continues to have a profound impact on their life long after a mentor is gone. It's good for us to be reminded about that. Sometimes even ten-minute conversations will have this ripple effect you cannot imagine." Many of us can recall mentors who spoke with us at just the right time and in just the right way, leaving significant legacies and sometimes even transforming our self-concepts.

Peta-Gaye Dixon, now a Student Success Mentor at LaGuardia Community College, recalls how two mentoring conversations led to her decision to pursue a career as a teacher. Entering LaGuardia intending to study business so she could support her mother back home in Jamaica, she never imagined herself in education because she had struggled with ADHD throughout her years of schooling:

> First, Lisa Silverman, my psychology professor, said, "Peta, your papers are terrific. Why don't you go into education?" I'm like, "Me, teaching children? I can't teach anybody. I barely made it through school. I can't do that." Professor Silverman replied, "Think about it." The next day I

got a copy of an email from her to a professor in the education department. It said, "I might have found you an excellent teacher candidate." I decided to follow Professor Silverman's advice so I went to see Professor Cornelia in education, who told me she also had ADHD. She sat me down in her office and showed me all her credentials on her wall, and she said, "I am you. And look where I am. You are going to be a great educator because you know what these kids are going through. You were that person in the back of the class that the teacher says can't do it." And then she asked me to sit down in her chair behind her desk, and she said, "You're in the professor's chair. That's your master's on the wall. That's your PhD. How are you going to tell me you can't do it? You're going to be a great teacher."

Not only did these two conversations with professors Silverman and Cornelia change the trajectory of Dixon's life, but they will also ripple through classrooms for years to come as she teaches and mentors her own students.

Mentoring conversations do not always begin during positive moments like the ones Dixon experienced when faculty encouraged her to dream big about her future. Karey Frink of Hope College had a powerful conversation when she felt she was on the brink of failure:

Chemistry was kicking my butt and I just had no idea what to do. And I got back the second exam and I thought, "Shoot! This is not going well. I need to get out." So I thought, "Well, it's either W or an F, so I will do a W." My professor, Dr. Peaslee, is a nuclear chemist and he is a wizard—super smart. He had heard that I might withdraw from chemistry, and he asked, "Why don't we talk?" I was shaking in my boots—I have to confront my super smart professor and tell him that I'm failing chemistry. But he really spoke to where he saw my strengths and said, "Karey, there are people in that classroom that were born to be in a lab; it clicks with them. But that might not be you and that's okay. Because where I see you being strong is having skills that others in the class don't have—like communication skills—understanding the basics of how science works and being able to communicate it in layman's terms." Ultimately, I ended up being a communication major, and that decision, I think, was provoked by the words of affirmation that Dr. Peaslee gave me that day.

As these stories and countless others from our interviews demonstrate, mentoring conversations matter, sometimes for a lifetime.

* * *

Given the potential power of frequent mentoring conversations at colleges and universities, everyone on campus might benefit from reflecting on these questions:

Am I using formal and informal moments to meaningfully engage with others?

Am I really listening to what I am hearing, listening to understand rather than to respond?

Am I taking the time to offer practical knowledge and guidance, or encouragement and support, to those who need it?

Am I using my personal connections to introduce students or colleagues to others who might be mentors to them?

Am I helping to create structures on campuses that will ensure more students are engaged in mentoring conversations?

What am I learning about myself from these relationships?

These consciousness-raising questions will help foster strong cultures that encourage mentoring conversations on campus.

Conclusion

The Future Is Relationship Rich

Even in the robot age—or perhaps, especially in the robot age—what matters is other people.

—Joseph Aoun, *Robot Proof: Higher Education in the Age of Artificial Intelligence*

Both of us have been fortunate to have had relationships with professors who made indelible impressions on us as first-year students. For Leo, it happened in James Scholes' American literature class at SUNY Geneseo, and for Peter, in Joan Klug's first-year philosophy course at Marquette. Both of these faculty members took the time to provide us with discerning feedback, encouraged us in our potential as writers, and then told us that we were capable of even better work. They did so with a perfect blend of challenge, critique, and affection. These were greater gifts to us than we could fully appreciate at the time, and they expanded our understandings of our own capabilities. Decades later those conversations with Jim and Joan remain milestones in our lives.

A central premise of this book is that as alumni look back on their undergraduate experiences, what they will value most about college are the relationships they formed—the *people* who afforded them a sense of belonging, helped shape their professional and personal identities, and guided them in discerning their purpose in the world and the values that are most meaningful to them. They will remember specific individuals—professors, student life staff, coaches, peers, and others—who unleashed their intellectual curiosity and taught them to be confident and critical. They will remember important conversations and lightning-bolt moments when truths were revealed . . . encouraging words or supportive hugs when they felt most vulnerable . . . staff members who knew them well, including, sometimes, their secret fears and hopes . . . peers who were inspirations or rivals . . . interactions with remarkable people in new cultures and contexts during study abroad experiences, internships, or community-based research . . . and long conversations in coffee shops or parking lots. Whenever we have listened to alumni who have returned to campus to accept awards or address audiences, the heart of their message inevitably honors the people in college who listened to them, encouraged them, challenged them, and mentored them.

Yet those of us who work in higher education often do not tell new students how much relationships matter in college; nor are our institutions designed to ensure that every student experiences the benefits of a relationship-rich education. Instead we fall into the trap of talking to students about college in transactional language (how to negotiate the maze of general education requirements, when to declare a major, where to register for courses, what minimum grade point average is required to participate in sorority rush) rather than helping them think about another type of pathway through college, an intentional journey that is defined by the relationships formed with faculty, staff, and peers that will make college meaningful, even transformational.

So how do we make relationship-rich undergraduate education a cultural priority and a practical reality on our campuses? How would higher education be different if we examined our policies and practices through the lens of relationships? How can institutions and all individuals within institutions act to make this happen? In this concluding chapter, we offer ten insights based on our interviews with nearly four hundred people on twenty-nine campuses. Students spoke passionately about relationships that have left lasting impressions on them. Many of the faculty, staff, and administrators told us that the personal and professional satisfaction they derived from deep connections with students continued to inspire their work in higher education day after day, despite challenges and resource constraints on every campus. We are grateful for the treasure trove of wisdom that they shared.

1. Institutions Must Act

Institutions must take the lead in creating relationship-rich undergraduate education and help students develop the capability to build constellations of mentors. The formal and informal customs, traditions, practices, and mores of higher education often feel mysterious and intimidating to new college students. In fact, these components of higher education may feel like a set of hidden codes to first-generation college students, who have not benefited from years of informal (and, for some, formal) advising, coaching, and exposure to collegespeak. These codes are often absorbed by students with a family history of college as if by osmosis, putting these students at an advantage on campus. Students who do not hear the messages about the importance of cultivating relationships—and how to go about doing so—will be seriously shortchanged.

Institutions can do more to explicitly emphasize the significance of building relationships and seeking mentors in college. Presidents and other campus leaders can underscore this message in addresses to new students, leveraging the power of stories. First-year seminar instructors can walk new students through the process of how to build academic relationships: speak to faculty after class, take advantage of office hours, approach faculty with whom they share academic interests about joining research teams, initiate meaningful conversations with staff and fellow students on a regular basis, and use advising time to talk about bigger goals and questions rather than routine, transactional matters. Student life staff can provide challenging and supportive feedback about student participation and leadership in campus clubs and organizations. Faculty can redesign large courses to make active learning and peer mentors central to students' success. Most important of all, institutional leaders—trustees, administrators, faculty, and staff—need to address basic questions such as: Do meaningful relationships with students really matter on our campus? How are we rewarding those who mentor, advise, and support students? How can we support and encourage everyone on campus to join in a culture encouraging students to seek meaningful relationships and mentors?

Every individual on campus can indeed make a personal difference in building that culture. The first step is for every individual, including professors, deans, student life professionals, dining hall staff, campus police—*everyone*—to raise their consciousness about the personal power they hold to make a difference in the lives of students by demonstrating welcome, care, and openness.

2. Relationships Matter, Especially for Those Who Are Marginalized

Designing for welcome and inclusion is good for all students. But relationships are especially powerful for students who for any reason might feel they are on the margins of higher education, including first-generation students, people of color, and LGBTQIA people. At our institution, Elon University, we have been inspired by Odyssey Scholars, a program for students who are civically engaged, action-oriented leaders in their communities and who are also predominantly first generation and demonstrate high financial need. Odyssey Scholars receive financial assistance, including funding for a study-away experience. And while financial aid is key, other dimensions of the program are perhaps more critical to students' success: strong mentoring by faculty and staff, effective peer mentoring, a programmatic culture of high expectations and campus involvement, and precollege orientation that promotes a sense of belonging. The Odyssey program's leadership can tap into special funds to help students with urgent needs and emergencies—hurdles that may derail success. The outcomes are impressive. Odyssey students graduate at a rate higher than the student body as a whole, participate in enriching experiences such as undergraduate research and study abroad at a higher rate than the general student body, are visible leaders on campus (including most recently as student body president), and have outstanding options upon graduation for advanced study or employment. As in CUNY's Accelerated Study in Associate Programs and Nevada State's Nepantla Program, the critical combination of wraparound support even prior to beginning college, high expectations for success, involvement in high-impact practices, and especially not leaving relationships to chance, leads to success. It matters that every student is known. It matters that each student's gifts and talents are valued and developed. It matters that each student receives the appropriate balance of challenge and support.

Why, therefore, is our system of higher education not designed to provide an Odyssey-like experience—a cohort characterized by strong relationships and high expectation for success—for every undergraduate student? Yes, this kind of education may have additional costs, but the costs pale in comparison to higher attrition rates, greater likelihood of student loan default, and the huge social costs of students not reaching their full potentials. Indeed, an analysis of CUNY's ASAP shows that "for each dollar of investment in ASAP by taxpayers, the return was $3 to $4."[1] The many programs and practices featured in this volume hold promise for strengthening undergraduate education, but big gaps remain in making sure that every student is connected to meaningful relationships in college. We can do far better.

What is called for is convening conversations about how to make relationship-rich practices and experiences accessible for every student. These conversations need to take place at the system and institution level in programs and departments, and among groups of like-minded academic citizens. This is not easy work, but to make it happen is entirely possible. These conversations will challenge reward systems and assumptions about curriculum, require new classroom practices, disrupt students' preconceived notions about what is important in college, and require everyone on campus to commit to cultural change. And all of these conversations and changes will require strong voices of leadership from presidents, provosts, faculty, staff, students, and governance leaders. This is the responsibility of everyone in higher education.

3. Classrooms Are Key

The classroom remains the most important place on campus for meaningful relationships to take root. To take nothing away from powerful opportunities students have to develop relationships outside of class (in residence halls, athletics, student life, campus employment, and more), if institutions want to make relationship-rich undergraduate education a priority, we recommend that they start in the classroom.

We love Rutgers-Newark Professor Sadia Abbas's conception of the classroom as "an unfolding conversation of three months." But if classrooms are to be places of meaningful interaction and deep learning, institutions must examine basic questions about faculty and pedagogy. Will the faculty whom students meet in first-year classes be available for longer-term relationships, or will they be gone from campus at the end of the term? Are students encountering teachers early in their undergraduate careers who make it a priority to form relationships with them? Do institutions support faculty development to encourage active learning practices in the classroom that lead to the likelihood of stronger student-faculty and student-student interactions? Even for institutions that offer online or face-to-face classes enrolling hundreds of students, are course redesign efforts supported to incorporate the use of learning assistants to increase the chances that students will form strong peer relationships in their education? How is high-quality relational teaching valued, celebrated, and rewarded?

We are realists. We understand that not all faculty members will have long-term relationships with their institutions or have teaching loads sufficiently manageable for them to spend as much time as they would like with students. And other priorities, such as research productivity, matter in higher education. But we believe that if relationship-rich undergraduate education is truly a priority (and not simply a public relations slogan), then the classroom-focused questions posed above need to be addressed directly and honestly at every level of the institution. We have borne witness to efforts on many campuses where good people rolled up their sleeves and got to work to strengthen undergraduate education in innovative ways, even when the environment to support change was far from perfect.

4. Mentoring Conversations Must Be Natural and Daily Occurrences

Students should have meaningful conversations everywhere across campus. Those of us who work in higher education need to be mindful of the resonance of these interactions, no matter how brief they may be, and make sure that all students have significant engagements with faculty and staff. Steve Grande, director of service learning at James Madison University, recently told us that each day he tries to remember how much his words impact students, even in casual and passing exchanges. We should all be so self-aware. Small moments matter a great deal. A campus that empowers all its faculty and staff to engage students with awareness and genuine humility will take major strides toward creating a relationship-rich environment. While formal mentoring programs matter, they are often insufficient in the number of students they touch, and the solution is not necessarily to create even more programs. A campus culture that nurtures relationships everywhere—from the classroom to the cafeteria and the residence hall to the dance studio—has the potential to immerse every student in a relationship-rich environment.

Everyone in higher education must be attentive to students who are not engaging, who are standing on the sidelines, who do not feel as though they have permission or the capacity to jump into campus life with both feet. We recall Timothy Eatman's statement "I am your professor" to a student he had just met, assuring her of his accessibility because they were citizens of the same institution. Imagine how different campuses might feel if more people followed Eatman's example. Everyone needs to take on the role of being an active presence in students' educations.

5. Relationships Are Everyone's Job

It takes everyone working together to create a relationship-rich campus. There is a base of relational education taking place on every campus we visited, with committed champions leading the way. We acknowledge that many of the practices included in this volume require extra time and thought, but there is potential for everyone on campus—all ranks of faculty and staff, as well as student leaders—to make a contribution to further enrich campus culture and strengthen programs.

As we did in our previous book, *The Undergraduate Experience*, we contend that institutions already have many substantial building blocks in place to form a more comprehensive culture of relationship-rich undergraduate education.[2] These include a cadre of leaders committed to furthering this culture—faculty willing to connect in the classroom, students willing to serve as peer mentors, and all those invested in the training and development work that undergirds these efforts. These individuals form a solid foundation upon which to build.

We recommend that institutions and individuals build on this base by asking Who is not being served? Which students are disconnected and most likely to leave? Where are our institutional weak spots? Florida International University's success with its Gateway Project is the perfect example of a team-based, data-driven effort to make substantial gains in student retention in first-year courses through relationship-rich practices. And the University of Iowa's Excelling@Iowa dares to ask the most basic questions about who the institution is not engaging and might be at risk of losing. We believe that institutions willing to bring important questions like these to the forefront of institutional planning will effect profound change if they stay the course.

6. Look beyond Your Peer Institutions for Examples of Good Practice

Everyone in higher education has much to learn about relationship-rich education from institutions outside their respective sectors. Those in community and technical colleges, research universities, liberal arts institutions, and comprehensive institutions can learn from those in other kinds of institutions. Those in exclusively or primarily face-to-face institutions can learn from those in online education, and vice versa. Innovative practices exist everywhere, and we should look beyond our existing peers for inspiration.

In January 2019 we caught up with President Scott Evenbeck of CUNY's Stella and Charles Guttman Community College, one of the most innovative community colleges in the nation, just as a session of the Association of American Colleges and

Universities annual meeting had concluded. He was red-faced with frustration. The session presenter had begun the program by polling the audience about the types of institutions they represented but failed to ask if anyone from community colleges might be present in the room—despite the fact that 38 percent of American college students attend community colleges! We share this story because it illustrates that all of us in higher education are too often unaware of (and perhaps too snobby to show interest in) the exemplary work taking place at institutions far different from our own. After visiting the Persistence Project at Oakton Community College and the peer mentoring programs at LaGuardia Community College, we were reminded of David Scobey's wise words: "Innovation often flows up the higher education status ladder." To prepare campuses for what America will look like in 2030 and beyond, those of us in higher education must break out of our comfortable patterns of engagement and study the inspiring and groundbreaking work currently taking place on a diverse range of campuses. We came away from our visits at many campuses with deep admiration for cultures of student success and commitment to students who will comprise the new American majority.

7. You Already Have a Foundation upon Which to Build

Developing more relational experiences for students may not require creating new programs but rather involve focusing on the strengths of existing programs and investing resources to make them even more available to all students. This requires time and commitment and the urge to resist chasing the next new thing. For example, writing programs are high-impact sites for relational learning, and most institutions are already doing good work in this regard. Across the country, writing programs like the Writing Fellows at Brown and Writing Coaches at Southern New Hampshire University refuse to frame themselves as transactional operations where students can get basic help fixing comma splices and split infinitives. Instead, the relational nature of learning and the human process of writing are treated with as much importance as the conceptual, organizational, and technical aspects of writing. Many institutions have other relationship-rich resources (first-year experience courses, learning communities, student organizations, honors programs, undergraduate research opportunities, capstone experiences, student employment, campus rec, and more) that could be adapted or expanded to reach even more students. Indeed, the right question might be How can every department on campus move from transactional practices toward relational ones? This is as relevant for academic departments as it is for the library, student life, academic support, physical plant, and virtually every other dimension of campus.

8. All Faculty Are Important to the Relationship-Rich Campus

Adjunct faculty play a vital role in the educational experiences of many students, but too often institutions do not treat them as essential partners in creating a relationship-rich campus. Since more than half of the faculty in the United States are adjuncts, colleges and universities must draw on the assets of these faculty to engage all students.[3]

Greg Hodges, vice president for academic and student success services at Patrick Henry Community College in Virginia, understands the importance of adjunct faculty: "While we have incredible student support personnel on our campus, if you take all of those services combined, it doesn't begin to scratch the surface of the amount of time a student spends in the classroom. On a community college campus, what happens in the classroom—including classrooms led by adjunct faculty—is candidly where everything either lives or dies." Several years ago, the college was in pursuit of a major Achieving the Dream grant, based upon the premise that "improving student success on a substantial scale requires colleges to engage in bold, holistic, sustainable institutional change." Patrick Henry's plans re-envisioned the support for adjunct faculty, who comprise a large proportion of its faculty workforce. Hodges recalls that President Angeline Godwin was so committed to this work that she proposed they continue whether the college got the grant funding or not: "This is not ancillary to what we do. This is what we do. If we are not doing this, we are not serving students." Happily, they won the funding.

Hodges describes the adjunct support initiatives that they launched as "relationship building 101," insisting that "none of it is rocket science." First, they built a learning management site where adjunct faculty could have access to a consolidated set of information vital to faculty and student success, ranging from the routine (Where can I make copies? How do I get new white board markers?) to the critical (How do I connect my students to key support services such as tutoring, the food pantry, and the clothing closet?). Further, they established an adjunct faculty mentoring program, in which each adjunct is paired with a full-time faculty colleague, usually in the same discipline, to encourage regular communication and mutual support—recognizing that adjuncts, who often are working full time in industry, bring distinct professional expertise to the college. Knowing that having places to meet students before and after class is also critical, the college designed spaces in two major classroom buildings for adjuncts to use while on campus, providing not only convenient spots to meet students but also access to essential tools such as computers, printers, and coffee.

Patrick Henry Community College offers an important lesson about weaving adjunct faculty into the fabric of campus life. Relationship-rich environments depend on all faculty members being empowered to do their best work with students, and yet in too many instances adjunct faculty lack even the fundamental information, tools, and relationships required to do their jobs effectively.

9. Stories about the Relationship-Rich Campus Are Powerful; Tell Them

In today's assessment-driven world of higher education, stories about the importance of relationships in college are the best way to describe the good work taking place on our campuses. Institutional data matter, but numbers alone do not capture the fullness of the undergraduate experience, so we need to integrate quantitative assessments with qualitative narratives to illustrate and enliven the stories we tell about the results and the value of higher education.[4] We need to tell these stories on campus and also to the public at large because the popular understanding of college is often incomplete and distorted.

In national and local media, coverage of exemplary undergraduate education is being swamped by entirely different messages questioning the importance of college and the experiences of students. A recent national survey concludes that "as in previous years, satisfaction with higher education is low," with only about one-third of Americans believing "higher education is fine the way it is."[5] The public narrative about higher education is dominated by tales of admissions and athletics scandals that touch only a tiny fraction of universities, hyperbolic arguments about political indoctrination, and often misleading reports about college costs and student loan debt. Each of these issues matters, but none tells the whole story. We in higher education need to reclaim the narrative by telling the powerful stories of how the *people* of our colleges and universities are making *the pivotal difference* in helping our students reach their potentials and how this, in turn, will allow our communities and our society to thrive. Stories of the transformational power of relationships are essential to rebuilding public trust in higher education.

In the daily stress and commotion of running complicated educational institutions, faculty and staff need to be reminded of the profound difference they make in the lives of students. Without such regular prompts, it is easy to fall back into routine patterns of transactional behavior. The stories about the consequences of deep human connections in college that we have shared in this volume (and hundreds more we gathered but did not include) inspired us. We know that others, too, in higher education have their own versions of these stories. Every day in our classrooms and across our campuses, students see new vistas, have curiosity sparked, find belonging and purpose, overcome despair and fear, improve prospects for families and communities, and rekindle hopes for the future. And, in the memorable words of Georgetown's Randy Bass, at every college and university, faculty and staff are working "effing hard" to make that possible. We need to uncover, tell, and honor these stories to remind all of us that relationships are at the core of undergraduate education.

10. Students Want Us to Know Them

On every campus we visited, we heard about the power of asking students "How are you?" and then genuinely listening to what they have to say. Students value this simple human-to-human connection more than those of us in higher education often fully appreciate, and these connections sometimes resonate for decades in ways we cannot fully comprehend.

Stopping to ask students how they are doing is hardly an innovative practice, but we heard over and over from students how much simple interactions matter. When the person asking this question took a minute to practice the art of generous listening, students felt that they mattered. Students are not necessarily asking others to solve their problems for them, but they do appreciate having their questions, insights, and concerns listened to with humility and care. No matter how long faculty, staff, and administrators have been at an institution, they know they do not always fully comprehend the complexity of students' lives, the trials they are facing, the stresses they are under, or the doubts they feel. But students told us over and over that it meant so much when a caring person took a few minutes to listen to them and how magical it was when a mentor helped them understand that they had something important to offer the world.

Learning, at its heart, is a relational process.

* * *

Relationships have the power to be transformational for individuals, for our institutions, and for our world. Many of us who have the rare and special privilege to work on a college campus believe that our most important legacies are the students we influence throughout our careers. None of us can know the number of lives we touch in our work with students nor the far-reaching consequences of our words and actions.

We wrote this book because we believe passionately in the power of higher education to transform lives, families, communities, and the world. The students we teach today will be citizens and leaders in 2050—just thirty years from now—when the earth's population will have grown to nearly ten billion. How will people be fed? Will there be sufficient clean water? What will the climate be like? Will the world's religions steer us toward peace or conflict? Will democracy endure? Relationship-rich undergraduate education will nurture the hearts, minds, and spirits of the leaders and citizens who will have to answer those questions. We cannot think of more important work than to prepare our students for that future with all the wisdom and compassion we have to offer.

Postscript in a Pandemic

Soon after we completed the final manuscript for this book, "the world turned upside down," to quote a song from *Hamilton*. The COVID-19 global pandemic forced colleges and universities to close their physical campuses, move all instruction online, and cancel commencements and other academic rites of spring.

The crisis also starkly highlighted the plight of students who do not have safe, stable homes and who lack basic resources such as food and Wi-Fi to sustain living and learning. COVID-19 is a powerful reminder that educational institutions—from pre-schools to universities—are not only places for learning and growth; they are also the bedrock for many students' physical, emotional, and spiritual well-being—and for some of the most important relationships in their lives.

From our own personal experiences interacting remotely with our students, colleagues, and extended families during these past weeks of isolation and social distancing, we feel deeply the loss of sustained, authentic human connection. The sense of loss is real for many educators, not just those of us working on residential campuses.

Faculty, staff, and students have strived to make remote education engaging and meaningful. Sometimes that has happened as we Zoom into classes, meetings, and happy hours to learn and work and laugh together. Despite our best efforts, we often miss the in-between times that have all but disappeared—the friendly exchange in the hallway, the casual chat with the people nearby before a class or meeting begins, the morning smile and greeting in the coffee shop. We find ourselves longing for routine interactions that we now see as glue holding our days together.

These past few weeks have reminded us of Janice M. McCabe's excellent book, *Connecting in College: How Friendship Networks Matter for Academic and Social Success*.* McCabe describes four underlying factors in undergraduate friendships that contribute to student success (and, we suspect, faculty and staff success, too):

1. intellectual engagement;
2. emotional support;
3. instrumental assistance, to help figure out how to get things done; and
4. competition, to motivate study and play.

The sudden shift to remote instruction and work ripped these underpinnings from beneath all of us. McCabe's analysis also reveals that the "academic multiplex ties" that integrate these four factors—when a shared cup of coffee turns into both emotional and instrumental support—are the foundation of many significant relationships for undergraduates. Our current experience with remote teaching suggests that we have taken for granted how face-to-face education enables these four factors to be woven together in the learning and lives of students—and the enormity of the vacuum that exists when our lives are forced out of our familiar ways of interacting.

In the midst of the seismic shift to remote instruction these past weeks, we have often reflected upon many of the interviews we conducted for this book with faculty, staff, and students who are part of Southern New Hampshire University's 90,000-student online campus. Erin Perry Schreier, the director of academic

---

* Janice M. McCabe, *Connecting in College: How Friendship Networks Matter for Academic and Social Success* (Chicago: University of Chicago Press, 2016).

support at SNHU, told us: "One of the biggest hurdles our students have to overcome is the feeling of being adrift in online classes where they don't get to see each other face-to-face and when they can't go up to their instructor to say, 'I'm really struggling with this' or 'I'm excited I've learned that.'" In such a seemingly impersonal environment, SNHU's president, Paul LeBlanc, insists that the "secret sauce" required for student success is that "there has to be someone who communicates to each student that they matter and that their education matters."

Those people at SNHU are the academic advisors and writing coaches who use the power of the human voice to cultivate meaningful and sustained connections with students through regular, frequent telephone conversations with the same students over multiple semesters. We return to Kayleigh Guzel's vivid description of the writing coach role: "Students are essentially alone in the cloud. They have discussion boards where they can interact with peers and they have e-mail, but the only human voice they hear are ours and their academic advisor's. So, we are able to be the human. That's what we do."

Indeed, "being the human" has been a rallying cry for faculty and staff trying to interact meaningfully with students during remote learning. Relationship-rich education may be hard to achieve online and certainly does require intentionality, yet it is even more urgent now than ever before. As we demonstrate throughout this book, decades of research make clear that positive human interactions are fundamental both to individual students achieving their own learning and educational goals, and to institutional priorities, including retention and graduation rates.

These past weeks have also reminded us of how much students on *every* campus we visited for this book value hearing the question How are you? If asked genuinely, and the response is listened to intently, that interaction can mean the world to students. A simple "how are you?" is sometimes a lifeline to a student in a moment of crisis, and at other times that question is the genesis of a lasting relationship. We find ourselves asking this question often during the pandemic, and we can hardly wait to get back to saying those words face-to-face.

As we write in April 2020, we are only beginning to see some of the implications of COVID-19 for students, faculty, staff, and colleges and universities. The pandemic surely will inflict serious personal, professional, and institutional damage, changing the academy for years to come. However, the past several weeks also forcefully underscore that relationships are the beating heart of higher education and that learning and well-being are intimately, inseparably connected. No matter the future, let us challenge ourselves to make relationship-rich education a reality for all of our students.

Notes

Foreword

1. Jan Arminio, Vasti Torres, and Raechele L. Pope, eds., *Why Aren't We There Yet? Taking Personal Responsibility for Creating an Inclusive Campus* (Sterling, VA: Stylus Publishing, 2012), 20.

2. "Connectedness and Health: The Science of Social Connection," Center for Compassion and Altruism Research and Education, May 9, 2014, http://ccare .stanford.edu/uncategorized/connectedness-health-the-science-of-social-connection -infographic/.

Introduction

1. Rebecca D. Cox, *The College Fear Factor: How Students and Professors Misunderstand One Another* (Cambridge, MA: Harvard University Press, 2009); John R. Thelin, *A History of American Higher Education*, 3rd ed. (Baltimore: Johns Hopkins University Press, 2019).

2. Lorelle L. Espinosa et al., "Race and Ethnicity in Higher Education: A Status Report," American Council on Education, 2019, https://vtechworks.lib.vt .edu/handle/10919/89187.

3. "Community College FAQs," Community College Research Center, Teachers College, Columbia University, n.d., https://ccrc.tc.columbia.edu /Community-College-FAQs.html.

4. Gail O. Mellow, "Opinion: The Biggest Misconception about Today's College Students," *New York Times*, August 28, 2017, https://www.nytimes.com /2017/08/28/opinion/community-college-misconception.html. For the most recent data, see the website for National Student Clearinghouse Research Center, https://nscresearchcenter.org/.

5. Sara Goldrick-Rab et al., "Still Hungry and Homeless in College," Wisconsin Hope Lab, University of Wisconsin–Madison, April 2018, https://hope4college .com/wp-content/uploads/2018/09/Wisconsin-HOPE-Lab-Still-Hungry-and -Homeless.pdf.

6. American College Health Association, National College Health Assessment II, Undergraduate Student Reference Group Data Report (Fall 2018), 31, accessed

July 25, 2019, https://www.acha.org/documents/ncha/NCHA-II_Fall_2018 _Undergraduate_Reference_Group_Data_Report.pdf.

7. Laura I. Rendón and Richard O. Hope, *Educating a New Majority: Transforming America's Educational System for Diversity* (San Francisco: Jossey-Bass, 1996).

8. Adrianna J. Kezar, ed., *Recognizing and Serving Low-Income Students in Higher Education: An Examination of Institutional Policies, Practices, and Culture* (New York: Routledge, 2011); Stephen John Quaye and Shaun R. Harper, eds., *Student Engagement in Higher Education: Theoretical Perspectives and Practical Approaches for Diverse Populations*, 2nd ed. (New York: Routledge, 2014); Tara J. Yosso, "Whose Culture Has Capital? A Critical Race Theory Discussion of Community Cultural Wealth," *Race Ethnicity and Education* 8, no. 1 (March 1, 2005): 69–91, https://doi.org/10.1080/1361332052000341006.

9. "State of Conflict," *Chronicle of Higher Education*, April 27, 2018, https:// www.chronicle.com/interactives/state-of-conflict.

10. Michael S. Roth, *Safe Enough Spaces: A Pragmatist's Approach to Inclusion, Free Speech, and Political Correctness on College Campuses* (New Haven, CT: Yale University Press, 2019).

11. Alexander W. Astin, *Four Critical Years* (San Francisco: Jossey-Bass, 1977); Vincent Tinto, *Leaving College: Rethinking the Causes and Cures of Student Attrition* (Chicago: University of Chicago Press, 1987); Matthew J. Mayhew et al., *How College Affects Students*, vol. 3: *21st Century Evidence That Higher Education Works* (San Francisco: Jossey-Bass, 2016).

12. Adrianna Kezar and Dan Maxey, "Faculty Matter: So Why Doesn't Everyone Think So?" *Thought & Action* 30 (2014): 31.

13. "Great Jobs, Great Lives: The 2014 Gallup-Purdue Index Report," Gallup and Purdue University, 2014, https://www.gallup.com/file/services/176768 /GallupPurdueIndex_Report_2014.pdf.

14. W. Brad Johnson, *On Being a Mentor: A Guide for Higher Education Faculty*, 2nd ed. (New York: Routledge, 2016); George D. Kuh and Ken O'Donnell, *Ensuring Quality and Taking High-Impact Practices to Scale* (Washington, DC: Association of American Colleges and Universities, 2013).

15. Cox, *College Fear Factor*, 13.

16. We will synthesize the existing research throughout the book. If you would like a comprehensive overview, start with Mayhew et al., *How College Affects Students*.

Chapter 1. Visions of the Possible

1. Estela Mara Bensimon, "The Underestimated Significance of Practitioner Knowledge in the Scholarship on Student Success," *Review of Higher Education* 30, no. 4 (June 21, 2007): 441–69, https://doi.org/10.1353/rhe.2007.0032.

2. Terrell L. Strayhorn, *College Students' Sense of Belonging: A Key to Educational Success for All Students* (New York: Routledge, 2012), 18–23.

3. Lee J. Cuba et al., *Practice for Life: Making Decisions in College* (Cambridge, MA: Harvard University Press, 2016), 3.

4. Alexander W. Astin, *Four Critical Years* (San Francisco: Jossey-Bass, 1977), 223.

5. Bensimon, "Underestimated Significance."

6. Shaun R. Harper, "Peer Support for African American Male College Achievement: Beyond Internalized Racism and the Burden of 'Acting White,'" *Journal of Men's Studies* 14, no. 3 (June 1, 2007): 337–58, https://doi.org/10.3149/jms.1403.337.

7. Derrick R. Brooms, Jelisa Clark, and Matthew Smith, "Being and Becoming Men of Character: Exploring Latino and Black Males' Brotherhood and Masculinity through Leadership in College," *Journal of Hispanic Higher Education* 17, no. 4 (October 1, 2018): 317–31, https://doi.org/10.1177/1538192717699048.

8. Strayhorn, *College Students' Sense of Belonging*, 9.

9. "Great Jobs, Great Lives: The 2014 Gallup-Purdue Index Report," Gallup and Purdue University, 2014, 7, https://www.gallup.com/file/services/176768/GallupPurdueIndex_Report_2014.pdf.

10. Susan A. Ambrose et al., *How Learning Works: Seven Research-Based Principles for Smart Teaching* (John Wiley & Sons, 2010), 83.

11. Ambrose et al., 83–89.

12. Karen Kurotsuchi Inkelas et al., *Living-Learning Communities That Work: A Research-Based Model for Design, Delivery, and Assessment* (Sterling, VA: Stylus Publishing, 2018).

13. Tori Haring-Smith, "Changing Students' Attitudes: Writing Fellows Programs," in *Writing across the Curriculum: A Guide to Developing Programs*, ed. Susan H. McLeod and Margo Soven (Washington, DC: Sage, 1992), 123–31, https://wac.colostate.edu/docs/books/mcleod_soven/mcleod_soven.pdf.

14. Vincent Tinto, *Leaving College: Rethinking the Causes and Cures of Student Attrition* (Chicago: University of Chicago Press, 1987), 181.

15. Roberta Espinoza, *Pivotal Moments: How Educators Can Put All Students on the Path to College* (Cambridge, MA: Harvard Education Press, 2011), 4.

16. W. Brad Johnson, "Mentoring: Make It a Constellation," *Brad Johnson's Blog Posts* (blog), January 14, 2014, http://www.wbradjohnson.com/news/2016/6/12/mentoring-make-it-a-constellation. See also W. Brad Johnson et al., "The Competence Constellation Model: A Communitarian Approach to Support Professional Competence," *Professional Psychology: Research and Practice* 44, no. 5 (October 2013): 343–54, https://doi.org/10.1037/a0033131.

17. Janice M. McCabe, *Connecting in College: How Friendship Networks Matter for Academic and Social Success* (Chicago: University of Chicago Press, 2016), 78.

18. Leo M. Lambert, Jason Husser, and Peter Felten, "Mentors Play Critical Role in Quality of College Experience, New Poll Suggests," *The Conversation*, August 22, 2018.

19. "Elon Poll: August 22, 2018," Elon University, accessed September 20, 2019, https://www.elon.edu/u/elon-poll/archive/2018-08-22/.

20. Vijay Kanagala, Laura Rendón, and Amaury Nora, "A Framework for Understanding Latino/a Cultural Wealth," website for Association of American Colleges and Universities, February 14, 2016, https://www.aacu.org/diversity democracy/2016/winter/kanagala.

21. Gloria Anzaldúa, *Borderlands: La Frontera: The New Mestiza*, 4th ed. (San Francisco: Aunt Lute Books, 2012).

22. On the importance of peer mentoring for Latinx students, see Roxanne V. Moschetti et al., "Peer Mentoring as Social Capital for Latina/o College Students at a Hispanic-Serving Institution," *Journal of Hispanic Higher Education* 17, no. 4 (October 1, 2018): 375–92, https://doi.org/10.1177/1538192717702949.

23. Espinoza, *Pivotal Moments*.

24. Sharon Daloz Parks, *Big Questions, Worthy Dreams: Mentoring Emerging Adults in Their Search for Meaning, Purpose, and Faith*, rev. ed. (San Francisco: Jossey-Bass, 2011), 211.

25. Parks, 201.

26. Richard J. Light, *Making the Most of College: Students Speak Their Minds*, rev. ed. (Cambridge, MA: Harvard University Press, 2004), 89.

27. Bret Eynon and Laura M. Gambino, eds., *Catalyst in Action: Case Studies of High-Impact EPortfolio Practice* (Sterling, VA: Stylus Publishing, 2018); Bret Eynon and Laura M. Gambino, *High Impact EPortfolio Practice: A Catalyst for Student, Faculty, and Institutional Learning* (Sterling, VA: Stylus Publishing, 2017).

28. William M. Sullivan, "Knowledge and Judgment in Practice as the Twin Aims of Learning," in *Transforming Undergraduate Education: Theory That Compels and Practices That Succeed*, ed. Donald W. Harward (Lanham, MD: Rowman & Littlefield, 2012), 143.

29. David Lopatto, *Science in Solution: The Impact of Undergraduate Research on Student Learning* (Tucson, AZ: Research Corporation for Science Advancement, 2009).

30. Maureen Vandermaas-Peeler, Paul C. Miller, and Jessie L. Moore, *Excellence in Mentoring Undergraduate Research* (Washington, DC: Council on Undergraduate Research, 2018), 43.

Chapter 2. Why Is This So Hard?

1. On this point, the results of our student interviews largely mirror chapter 2 in Rebecca D. Cox, *The College Fear Factor: How Students and Professors Misunderstand One Another* (Cambridge, MA: Harvard University Press, 2009).

2. Claude M. Steele, *Whistling Vivaldi: How Stereotypes Affect Us and What We Can Do*, reprint ed. (New York: W.W. Norton, 2011), 3.

3. Steele, 181.

4. Eileen Kogl Camfield, "Mediated-Efficacy: Hope for 'Helpless' Writers," *Journal of Developmental Education* 39, no. 3 (2016): 9.

5. Jerome Graham and Shannon McClain, "A Canonical Correlational Analysis Examining the Relationship between Peer Mentorship, Belongingness, Impostor Feelings, and Black Collegians' Academic and Psychosocial Outcomes," *American Educational Research Journal* 56, no. 6 (2019): 2333–67.

6. Tara J. Yosso, "Whose Culture Has Capital? A Critical Race Theory Discussion of Community Cultural Wealth," *Race Ethnicity and Education* 8, no. 1 (March 1, 2005): 69–91, https://doi.org/10.1080/1361332052000341006; Anthony Abraham Jack, *The Privileged Poor: How Elite Colleges Are Failing Disadvantaged Students* (Cambridge, MA: Harvard University Press, 2019).

7. Matthew C. Reeder and Neal Schmitt, "Motivational and Judgment Predictors of African American Academic Achievement at PWIs and HBCUs," *Journal of College Student Development* 54, no. 1 (February 2, 2013): 29–42, https://doi.org/10.1353/csd.2013.0006.

8. Jack, *The Privileged Poor*, 83.

9. Leslie Bayers and Eileen Camfield, "Student Shaming and the Need for Academic Empathy," *Hybrid Pedagogy*, April 5, 2018, http://hybridpedagogy.org/student-shaming-academic-empathy/; Brené Brown, "Shame Resilience Theory: A Grounded Theory Study on Women and Shame," *Families in Society* 87, no. 1 (January 1, 2006): 43–52, https://doi.org/10.1606/1044-3894.3483.

10. Anna Parkman, "The Imposter Phenomenon in Higher Education: Incidence and Impact," *Journal of Higher Education Theory and Practice* 16, no. 1 (2016), https://doi.org/10.33423/jhetp.v16i1.1936.

11. Parkman, 53.

12. Michelle Harris et al., *Stories from the Front of the Room: How Higher Education Faculty of Color Overcome Challenges and Thrive in the Academy* (Lanham, MD: Rowman & Littlefield, 2017); Adrianna Kezar, ed., *Embracing Non-Tenure Track Faculty: Changing Campuses for the New Faculty Majority* (New York: Routledge, 2012); Yonghong Jade Xu, "Gender Disparity in STEM Disciplines: A Study of Faculty Attrition and Turnover Intentions," *Research in Higher Education* 49, no. 7 (November 1, 2008): 607–24, https://doi.org/10.1007/s11162-008-9097-4.

13. Parkman, "Imposter Phenomenon in Higher Education."

14. Cox, *College Fear Factor*, 42.

15. Vincent Tinto, "Classrooms as Communities: Exploring the Educational Character of Student Persistence," *Journal of Higher Education* 68, no. 6 (November 1997): 599, https://doi.org/10.1080/00221546.1997.11779003.

16. M. Stains et al., "Anatomy of STEM Teaching in North American Universities," *Science* 359, no. 6383 (March 30, 2018): 1468, https://doi.org/10.1126/science.aap8892.

17. Daniel F. Chambliss and Christopher G. Takacs, *How College Works* (Cambridge, MA: Harvard University Press, 2014), 75.

18. Sara E. Brownell and Kimberly D. Tanner, "Barriers to Faculty Pedagogical Change: Lack of Training, Time, Incentives, and . . . Tensions with Professional Identity?" *CBE Life Sciences Education* 11, no. 4 (December 1, 2012): 339–46, https://doi.org/10.1187/cbe.12-09-0163; Erin E. Shortlidge and Sarah L. Eddy, "The Trade-Off between Graduate Student Research and Teaching: A Myth?," *PLOS ONE* 13, no. 6 (June 25, 2018): e0199576, https://doi.org/10.1371/journal .pone.0199576.

19. Matt Reed, "'I Wasn't Trained for This,'" Inside Higher Ed, accessed July 25, 2019, https://www.insidehighered.com/blogs/confessions-community -college-dean/%E2%80%9Ci-wasn%E2%80%99t-trained-%E2%80%9D.

20. Mary Wright et al., "Faculty Development Improves Teaching and Learning," *PODSpeaks* (blog), n.d., https://podnetwork.org/content/uploads /POD-Speaks-Issue-2_Jan2018-1.pdf.

21. Richard Arum and Josipa Roksa, *Academically Adrift: Limited Learning on College Campuses* (Chicago: University of Chicago Press, 2011).

22. Chambliss and Takacs, *How College Works*, 75.

23. Cathy N. Davidson, *The New Education: How to Revolutionize the University to Prepare Students for a World in Flux* (New York: Basic Books, 2017), 212.

24. Caroline Sotello Viernes Turner, Juan Carlos González, and J. Luke Wood, "Faculty of Color in Academe: What 20 Years of Literature Tells Us," *Journal of Diversity in Higher Education* 1, no. 3 (2008): 139–68, https://doi.org/10.1037 /a0012837.

25. Bradley E. Cox et al., "A Culture of Teaching: Policy, Perception, and Practice in Higher Education," *Research in Higher Education* 52, no. 8 (December 1, 2011): 808–29, https://doi.org/10.1007/s11162-011-9223-6.

26. Yosso, "Whose Culture Has Capital?"; Alexander W. Astin, *Are You Smart Enough? How Colleges' Obsession with Smartness Shortchanges Students* (Sterling, VA: Stylus Publishing, 2016).

Chapter 3. Making Relationships a Cultural Priority

1. Wade W. Nobles, *African Psychology: Toward Its Reclamation, Reascension, or Revitalization* (Oakland, CA: Institute for the Advanced Study of Black Family Life and Culture, 1986).

2. Alexander W. Astin, *Are You Smart Enough? How Colleges' Obsession with Smartness Shortchanges Students* (Sterling, VA: Stylus Publishing, 2016).

3. David Louis Schoem, Christine Modey, and Edward P. St. John, eds., *Teaching the Whole Student: Engaged Learning with Heart, Mind, and Spirit* (Sterling, VA: Stylus Publishing, 2017).

4. Schoem, Modey, and St. John, *Teaching the Whole Student*, 79.

5. Alexander W. Astin, Helen S. Astin, and Jennifer A. Lindholm, *Cultivating the Spirit: How College Can Enhance Students' Inner Lives* (San Francisco: Jossey-Bass, 2010), 1.

6. Lee J. Cuba et al., *Practice for Life: Making Decisions in College* (Cambridge, MA: Harvard University Press, 2016), 170.

7. Stan Van Ginkel et al., "Building a Vibrant Honors Community among Commuter Students," *Journal of the National Collegiate Honors Council* 13 (Fall/Winter 2012).

8. Parker J. Palmer, *The Courage to Teach: Exploring the Inner Landscape of a Teacher's Life*, 20th ed. (San Francisco: Jossey-Bass, 2017), 3.

9. Ken Bain, *What the Best College Teachers Do* (Cambridge, MA: Harvard University Press, 2004), 18.

10. American Academy of Arts and Sciences and Commission on the Future of Undergraduate Education, *The Future of Undergraduate Education: The Future of America* (Cambridge, MA: American Academy of Arts and Sciences, 2017), 12, https://www.amacad.org/multimedia/pdfs/publications/research papersmonographs/CFUE_Final-Report/Future-of-Undergraduate-Education .pdf.

11. Jerry G. Gaff and Leo M. Lambert, "Socializing Future Faculty to the Values of Undergraduate Education," *Change: The Magazine of Higher Learning* 28, no. 4 (August 1, 1996): 38–45, https://doi.org/10.1080/00091383.1996 .9937760.

12. Bob Chapman and Raj Sisodia, *Everybody Matters: The Extraordinary Power of Caring for Your People Like Family* (New York: Penguin, 2015), 67.

13. Chapman and Sisodia, 15.

14. Peter Felten et al., *The Undergraduate Experience: Focusing Institutions on What Matters Most* (San Francisco: Jossey-Bass, 2016), 59.

15. "Unsung Heroes," n.d., https://unsungheroes.org.

16. Challenge Success, "A 'Fit' Over Rankings: Why College Engagement Matters More Than Selectivity," Stanford Graduate School of Education, 2018, https://ed.stanford.edu/sites/default/files/challenge_success_white_paper_on _college_admissions_10.1.2018-reduced.pdf.

17. Lynn E. Swaner, "The Theories, Contexts, and Multiple Pedagogies of Engaged Learning," in *Transforming Undergraduate Education; Theory That Compels and Practices That Succeed*, ed. Donald W. Harward (Lanham, MD: Rowman & Littlefield, 2012), 85.

18. George Keller, *Transforming a College: The Story of a Little-Known College's Strategic Climb to National Distinction* (Baltimore: Johns Hopkins University Press, 2004).

19. "Elon Teacher-Scholar Statement," n.d., https://www.elon.edu/u/adminis tration/provost/elon-teacher-scholar-statement/.

20. Anne Bolin et al., "Recommendations of the Presidential Task Force on Scholarship," Elon University, November 2007, 29, https://cdm16128.contentdm.oclc.org/digital/collection/p16128coll1/id/0/rec/1.

Chapter 4. Creating Relationship-Rich Classrooms

1. David Schoem uses this same phrase in his chapter on "Relational Teaching and Learning" in *Teaching the Whole Student: Engaged Learning with Heart, Mind, and Spirit*, ed. David Schoem, Christine Modey, and Edward P. St. John (Sterling, VA: Stylus Publishing, 2017). See also Harriet L. Schwartz, *Connected Teaching: Relationships, Power, and Mattering in Higher Education* (Sterling, VA: Stylus Publishing, 2019).

2. "This I Believe: A Public Dialogue about Belief—One Essay at a Time," accessed December 19, 2019, https://thisibelieve.org/.

3. Karen A. Stout, "The Urgent Case: Focusing the Next Generation of Community College Redesign on Teaching and Learning" (Dallas Herring Lecture, Belk Center for Community College Leadership and Research, North Carolina State University, 2018), 5.

4. George D. Kuh et al., *What Matters to Student Success: A Review of the Literature* (Washington, DC: National Postsecondary Education Cooperative, 2006), 41. See also Young Kim and Linda J. Sax, "The Impact of College Students' Interactions with Faculty: A Review of General and Conditional Effects," in *Higher Education: Handbook of Theory and Research*, vol. 32, ed. Michael B. Paulsen (New York: Springer International, 2017), 85–139; Matthew J. Mayhew et al., *How College Affects Students*, vol. 3: *21st Century Evidence That Higher Education Works* (San Francisco: Jossey-Bass, 2016).

5. Adriana Kezar and Dan Maxey, "Faculty Matter: So Why Doesn't Everyone Think So?," *Thought & Action* 30 (2014); Carol A. Lundberg and Laurie A. Schreiner, "Quality and Frequency of Faculty-Student Interaction as Predictors of Learning: An Analysis by Student Race/Ethnicity," *Journal of College Student Development* 45, no. 5 (2004).

6. Chi Baik, Wendy Larcombe, and Abi Brooker, "How Universities Can Enhance Student Mental Wellbeing: The Student Perspective," *Higher Education Research & Development* 38, no. 4 (2019).

7. Roger G. Baldwin and Matthew R. Wawrzynski, "Contingent Faculty as Teachers: What We Know; What We Need to Know," *American Behavioral Scientist* 55, no. 11 (2011); Paul D. Umbach, "How Effective Are They? Exploring the Impact of Contingent Faculty on Undergraduate Education," *Review of Higher Education* 30, no. 2 (2007).

8. Di Xu, "Academic Performance in Community Colleges: The Influences of Part-Time and Full-Time Instructors," *American Education Research Journal* 56, no. 2 (2019).

9. National Center for Education Statistics, "Characteristics of Postsecondary Faculty," *Integrated Postsecondary Education Data System* (Washington, DC: Institute for Education Sciences, 2018), https://nces.ed.gov/programs/coe/indicator_csc.asp.

10. Kezar and Maxey, "Faculty Matter," 35.

11. Alicia Fedelina Chavez and Susan Diana Longerbeam, *Teaching across Cultural Strengths: A Guide to Balancing Integrated and Individuated Cultural Frameworks in College Teaching* (Sterling, VA: Stylus Publishing, 2016), 66.

12. Jeffrey F. Milem, "The Educational Benefits of Diversity: Evidence from Multiple Sectors," in *Compelling Interest: Examining the Evidence on Racial Dynamics in Colleges and Universities*, ed. Mitchell J. Chang et al. (Palo Alto, CA: Stanford University Press, 2003); Mitchell J. Chang et al., "The Educational Benefits of Sustaining Cross-Racial Interaction among Undergraduates," *Journal of Higher Education* 77, no. 3 (May 1, 2006): 430–55, https://doi.org/10.1080/00221546.2006.11778933.

13. Jan L. Arminio, Vasti Torres, and Raechele L. Pope, eds., *Why Aren't We There Yet? Taking Personal Responsibility for Creating an Inclusive Campus* (Sterling, VA: Stylus Publishing, 2012).

14. Laura I. Rendón, "Validating Culturally Diverse Students: Toward a New Model of Learning and Student Development," *Innovative Higher Education* 19, no. 1 (September 1, 1994): 33–51, https://doi.org/10.1007/BF01191156.

15. Laura I. Rendón Linares and Susana M. Muñoz, "Revisiting Validation Theory: Theoretical Foundations, Applications, and Extensions," *Enrollment Management Journal* (Summer 2011): 12–33.

16. M. Lee Upcraft, John N. Gardner, and Betsy O. Barefoot, eds., *Challenging and Supporting the First-Year Student: A Handbook for Improving the First Year of College* (San Francisco: Jossey-Bass, 2004).

17. Lee J. Cuba et al., *Practice for Life: Making Decisions in College* (Cambridge, MA: Harvard University Press, 2016), 3.

18. Hollace Graff, Eva M. de la Rive, and Joianne Smith, "Changing Our Teaching to Increase Student Engagement, Persistence, and Equity" (n.d.) unpublished research from Oakton Community College]; Elisabeth Barnett, "Faculty Leadership and Student Persistence: A Story From Oakton Community College," Community College Research Center, Teachers College, Columbia University, May 9, 2018, accessed September 17, 2019, https://ccrc.tc.columbia.edu/blog/faculty-leadership-student-persistence-oakton-community-college.html.

19. David Lopatto, *Science in Solution: The Impact of Undergraduate Research on Student Learning* (Tucson, AZ: Research Corporation for Science Advancement, 2009); Maureen Vandermaas-Peeler, Paul C. Miller, and Jessie L. Moore, *Excellence in Mentoring Undergraduate Research* (Washington, DC: Council on Undergraduate Research, 2018).

20. Katelyn M. Cooper et al., "What's in a Name? The Importance of Students Perceiving That an Instructor Knows Their Names in a High-Enrollment Biology Classroom," *CBE Life Sciences Education* 16, no. 1 (2017): 7.

21. For an overview of psychological efficacy interventions, see Gregory M. Walton and Timothy D. Wilson, "Wise Interventions: Psychological Remedies for Social and Personal Problems," *Psychology Review* 125, no. 5 (2018).

22. Linda B. Nilson, *Specifications Grading: Restoring Rigor, Motivating Students, and Saving Faculty Time* (Sterling, VA: Stylus Publishing, 2015).

23. Scott E. Carrell, Michal Kurlaender, and Monica P. Bhatt, "Experimental Evidence of Professor Engagement on Student Outcomes" (working paper, 2016), http://faculty.econ.ucdavis.edu/faculty/scarrell/engagement.pdf, 17.

24. Colleen Flaherty, "'My Professor Cares': Can 'Light-Touch, Targeted Feedback' to Students via Email Improve Their Perceptions of and Performance in a Class? New Research Says in Some Cases the Answer Is Yes," *Inside Higher Ed*, January 14, 2019.

25. Mayhew et al., *How College Affects Students*, 553; see also Jerome Graham and Shannon McClain, "A Canonical Correlational Analysis Examining the Relationship between Peer Mentorship, Belongingness, Imposter Feelings, and Black Collegians' Academic and Psychosocial Outcomes," *American Educational Research Journal* 56, no. 6 (2019), 2333–67.

26. Scott Freeman et al., "Active Learning Increases Student Performance in Science, Engineering, and Mathematics," *PNAS* 111, no. 23 (2014); M. K. Smith et al., "Why Peer Discussion Improves Student Performance on In-Class Concept Questions," *Science* 323, no. 5910 (2009); Eva Kyndt et al., "A Meta-Analysis of the Effects of Face-to-Face Cooperative Learning: Do Recent Studies Falsify or Verify Earlier Findings?" *Educational Research Review* 10 (2013).

27. Barbara J. Millis and Phillip G. Cottell, *Cooperative Learning for Higher Education Faculty* (Phoenix, AZ: Oryx, 1998).

28. Shannon B. Seidel and Kimberly D. Tanner, "'What If Students Revolt?': Considering Student Resistance: Origins, Options, and Opportunities for Investigation," *CBE Life Sciences Education* 12, no. 4 (December 1, 2013): 586–95, https://doi.org/10.1187/cbe-13-09-0190; Sneha Tharayil et al., "Strategies to Mitigate Student Resistance to Active Learning," *International Journal of STEM Education* 5, no. 1 (March 12, 2018): 7, https://doi.org/10.1186/s40594-018-0102-y; John Tagg, foreword to *Why Students Resist Learning: A Practical Model for Understanding and Helping Students*, reprint ed., ed. Anton O. Tolman and Janine Kremling (Sterling, VA: Stylus Publishing, 2016).

29. Sarah L. Eddy et al., "Caution, Student Experience May Vary: Social Identities Impact a Student's Experience in Peer Discussions," *CBE Life Sciences Education* 14, no. 4 (2015), https://www.lifescied.org/doi/pdf/10.1187/cbe.15-05 -0108.

30. Sat Gavassa et al., "Closing the Achievement Gap in a Large Introductory Course by Balancing Reduced In-Person Contact with Increased Course Structure," *CBE Life Sciences Education* 18, no. 1 (2019), https://www.lifescied.org/doi/full/10.1187/cbe.18-08-0153.

31. George Kuh, Ken O'Donnell, and Carol Geary Schneider, "HIPs at Ten," *Change: The Magazine of Higher Learning* 49, no. 5 (September 3, 2017): 8–16, https://doi.org/10.1080/00091383.2017.1366805.

32. Michele Eodice, Anne Ellen Geller, and Neal Lerner, *The Meaningful Writing Project: Learning, Teaching, and Writing in Higher Education* (Logan: Utah State University Press, 2017), 133.

33. bell hooks, *Teaching Critical Thinking: Practical Wisdom* (New York: Routledge, 2009), 43.

34. "#AmherstUprising: Why Student Protests Are Getting It Right," *Observer* (blog), November 19, 2015, https://observer.com/2015/11/amherstuprising-why-student-protests-are-getting-it-right/.

35. Kristen A. Renn, "Including All Voices in the Classroom: Teaching Lesbian, Gay, and Bisexual Students," *College Teaching* 48, no. 4 (October 1, 2000): 129–35, https://doi.org/10.1080/87567550009595829.

36. The website Being Human in Stem, accessed July 26, 2019, http://www.beinghumaninstem.com/.

37. Rebecca D. Cox, *The College Fear Factor: How Students and Professors Misunderstand One Another* (Cambridge, MA: Harvard University Press, 2009), 117.

38. Andrew J. Cavanagh et al., "Trust, Growth Mindset, and Student Commitment to Active Learning in a College Science Course," *CBE Life Sciences Education* 17, no. 1 (March 1, 2018): ar10, https://doi.org/10.1187/cbe.17-06-0107.

39. Kathleen Fitzpatrick, *Generous Thinking: A Radical Approach to Saving the University* (Baltimore: Johns Hopkins University Press, 2019), 213.

40. Marilyn S. Sternglass, *Time to Know Them: A Longitudinal Study of Writing and Learning at the College Level* (Mahwah, NJ: Lawrence Erlbaum, 1997); Eodice, Geller, and Lerner, *The Meaningful Writing Project*.

41. William Condon et al., *Faculty Development and Student Learning: Assessing the Connections* (Bloomington: Indiana University Press, 2016).

Chapter 5. Rich Relationships Everywhere

1. Valerie Otero, Steven Pollock, and Noah Finkelstein, "A Physics Department's Role in Preparing Physics Teachers: The Colorado Learning Assistant Model," *American Journal of Physics* 78, no. 11 (November 2010): 1218–24, https://doi.org/10.1119/1.3471291.

2. Learning Assistants Program, University of Colorado Boulder, n.d., https://www.colorado.edu/program/learningassistant/.

3. "College Faculty Have Become More Racially and Ethnically Diverse, but Remain Far Less So Than Students," *Pew Research Center* (blog), accessed August 1, 2019, https://www.pewresearch.org/fact-tank/2019/07/31/us-college -faculty-student-diversity/.

4. Erich N. Pitcher et al., "Affirming Policies, Programs, and Supportive Services: Using an Organizational Perspective to Understand LGBTQ+ College Student Success," *Journal of Diversity in Higher Education* 11, no. 2 (2018): 117–32, https://doi.org/10.1037/dhe0000048; Z Nicolazzo, *Trans* in College: Transgender Students' Strategies for Navigating Campus Life and the Institutional Politics of Inclusion* (Sterling, VA: Stylus Publishing, 2016); Carmen Cruz et al., "Peer Coaching Program Development: A Framework of First-Year Latina/o Student Persistence Pursuing STEM Pathways at a Hispanic Serving Institution," *Journal of Hispanic Higher Education*, August 2, 2019, 1538192719867096, https://doi.org/10.1177/1538192719867096; Kristen A. Renn and Karen D. Arnold, "Reconceptualizing Research on College Student Peer Culture," *Journal of Higher Education* 74, no. 3 (May 1, 2003): 261–91, https://doi.org/10.1080 /00221546.2003.11780847.

5. Alison Cook-Sather, Catherine Bovill, and Peter Felten, *Engaging Students as Partners in Learning and Teaching: A Guide for Faculty* (San Francisco: Jossey-Bass, 2014).

6. Gretchen Kreahling McKay, "Engaging the Nonart History Student: A Tale of Five Football Players (and Others) in Roman Art," in *Active Learning Strategies in Higher Education: Teaching for Leadership, Innovation, and Creativity*, ed. Anastasia Misseyanni et al. (Bingley, UK: Emerald Publishing, 2018), 187–209, https://doi.org/10.1108/978-1-78714-487-320181009.

7. Mark C. Carnes, *Minds on Fire: How Role-Immersion Games Transform College*, reprint ed. (Cambridge, MA: Harvard University Press, 2018).

8. Amy A. Overman, "Strategies for Group-Level Mentoring of Undergraduates: Creating a Laboratory Environment That Supports Publications and Funding," *Frontiers in Psychology* 10 (February 2019).

9. Megha Joshi, Melissa L. Aikens, and Erin L. Dolan, "Direct Ties to a Faculty Mentor Related to Positive Outcomes for Undergraduate Researchers," *BioScience* 69, no. 5 (2019): 389–97; Maureen Vandermaas-Peeler, Paul C. Miller, and Jessie L. Moore, *Excellence in Mentoring Undergraduate Research* (Washington, DC: Council on Undergraduate Research, 2018).

10. For more information about "the Daniel Lab," see http://faculty.washington .edu/danielt/research2016.html.

11. Conversation Center, Department of Rhetoric, University of Iowa (website), accessed July 31, 2019, https://clas.uiowa.edu/rhetoric/conversation-center.

12. Marybeth Gasman and Thai-Huy Nguyen, *Making Black Scientists: A Call to Action* (Cambridge, MA: Harvard University Press, 2019).

13. Rachel Fishman, Ernest Ezeugo, and Sophie Nguyen, "Varying Degrees 2018," New America (website), accessed July 31, 2019, https://www.newamerica.org/education-policy/reports/varying-degrees-2018/; Rodney Parks and Alexander Taylor, "Innovative Credentialing: Employers Weigh in on Co-Curricular Transcripts," *College and University* 91, no. 2 (2016): 63–72.

14. "Comprehensive Learner Profiles: Helping Faculty Improve Pedagogy in the Classroom," accessed July 31, 2019, https://er.educause.edu/blogs/2019/6/comprehensive-learner-profiles-helping-faculty-improve-pedagogy-in-the-classroom.

15. For an overview of equity and privacy issues, see "Predictive Analytics Are Boosting College Graduation Rates, but Do They Also Invade Privacy and Reinforce Racial Inequities?," *Hechinger Report* (blog), August 6, 2019, https://hechingerreport.org/predictive-analytics-boosting-college-graduation-rates-also-invade-privacy-and-reinforce-racial-inequities/.

16. Lori D. Patton, Shaun R. Harper, and Jessica Harris, "Using Critical Race Theory to (Re)Interpret Widely Studied Topics Related to Students in US Higher Education," in *Critical Approaches to the Study of Higher Education*, ed. Ana M. Martinez-Aleman, Brian Pusser, and Estela Mara Bensimon (Baltimore: Johns Hopkins University Press, 2015), 193–219.

17. David K. Kirk, "An Honors College That Honors Grit," *New York Times*, May 22, 2018, https://www.nytimes.com/2018/05/22/opinion/honors-college-rutgers.html. Hari Sreenivasan, "At This College, Academic Excellence Requires Passion for the Social Good," PBS Newshour, October 16, 2018, https://www.pbs.org/newshour/show/at-this-college-academic-excellence-requires-passion-for-the-social-good.

Chapter 6. Mentoring Conversations

1. W. Brad Johnson, *On Being a Mentor: A Guide for Higher Education Faculty*, 2nd ed. (New York: Routledge, 2016); Lois J. Zachary, *The Mentor's Guide: Facilitating Effective Learning Relationships*, 2nd ed. (San Francisco: Jossey-Bass, 2012); Peter Felten et al., *Transformative Conversations: A Guide to Mentoring Communities among Colleagues in Higher Education* (San Francisco: Jossey-Bass, 2013).

2. Johnson, *On Being a Mentor*.

3. Sharon Daloz Parks, *Big Questions, Worthy Dreams: Mentoring Emerging Adults in Their Search for Meaning, Purpose, and Faith*, rev. ed. (San Francisco: Jossey-Bass, 2011), 203–4.

4. Daniel F. Chambliss and Christopher G. Takacs, *How College Works* (Cambridge, MA: Harvard University Press, 2014), 155.

5. Zaretta Hammond, *Culturally Responsive Teaching and the Brain: Promoting Authentic Engagement and Rigor among Culturally and Linguistically Diverse Students* (Thousand Oaks, CA: Corwin, 2015).

6. Challenge Success, "A 'Fit' Over Rankings: Why College Engagement Matters More than Selectivity," Survey, Stanford University Graduate School of Education, October 2018, 2, http://www.challengesuccess.org/wp-content/uploads/2018/10/Challenge-Success-White-Paper-on-College-Admissions-October-2018.pdf.

7. Laurent A. Parks Daloz, foreword to *The Mentor's Guide: Facilitating Effective Learning Relationships*, 2nd ed., by Lois J. Zachary (John Wiley & Sons, 2012), xiii–xiv.

8. Torie Weiston-Serdan, *Critical Mentoring: A Practical Guide* (Sterling, VA: Stylus Publishing, 2017), 88–89.

9. Roberta Espinoza, *Pivotal Moments: How Educators Can Put All Students on the Path to College* (Cambridge, MA: Harvard Education Press, 2011).

10. Mary-Ann Winkelmes, Allison Boye, and Suzanne Tapp, eds., *Transparent Design in Higher Education Teaching and Leadership: A Guide to Implementing the Transparency Framework Institution-Wide to Improve Learning and Retention* (Sterling, VA: Stylus Publishing, 2019).

Conclusion. The Future Is Relationship Rich

Epigraph. Joseph Aoun, *Robot-Proof: Higher Education in the Age of Artificial Intelligence* (Cambridge, MA: MIT Press, 2017), 58.

1. Henry M. Levin and Emma Garcia, "Accelerating Community College Graduation Rates: A Benefit-Cost Analysis," *Journal of Higher Education* 89, no. 1 (2017): 1–27, https://doi.org/10.1080/00221546.2017.1313087.

2. Peter Felten et al., *The Undergraduate Experience: Focusing Institutions on What Matters Most* (San Francisco: Jossey-Bass, 2016).

3. Adrianna Kezar and Dan Maxey, "Faculty Matter: So Why Doesn't Everyone Think So?," *Thought & Action* 30 (2014): 29.

4. George D. Kuh, ed., *Using Evidence of Student Learning to Improve Higher Education* (San Francisco: Jossey-Bass, 2015).

5. Rachel Fishman et al., "Varying Degrees 2019," New America (website), September 11, 2019, 22, newamerica.org/education-policy/reports/varying-degrees-2019/.

Index